Introduction: Music for Youth

1 New friends ▸ p. 11

a) *What do you know about the new friends? Circle the right answer. You need the letters in brackets in part b).*

Asif

Katrina

Latisha

Robert

1 Katrina is from ...

Manchester. (P)	the Orkneys. (L)	London. (B)

2 Does Asif play in a band?

Yes. (J)	No. (M)	Don't know. (S)

3 The name of Asif's brother is ...

Ali. (E)	Ranjit. (H)	Hassan. (A)

4 Which instrument does Latisha play?

The steel drum. (C)	The fiddle. (U)	The keyboard. (F)

5 Is Robert in the festival?

Yes. (L)	No. (K)	Don't know. (P)

6 Robert is from ...

the USA. (R)	Australia. (T)	Canada. (E)

7 Who is a DJ back home?

Latisha. (I)	Asif. (E)	Robert. (E)

8 Does Robert play an instrument?

Yes. (R)	No. (C)	Don't know. (L)

9 Latisha is from ...

Birmingham. (E)	Manchester. (O)	London. (B)

10 Latisha loves ...

football. (W)	ice hockey. (G)	squash. (N)

11 In the evening the students go to watch ...

Katrina's fiddle band. (M)	Latisha's steel drum band. (K)	Hassan's Asian Fusion band. (B)

b) *Now write the letters next to your answers in the boxes. If your answers are correct, the letters make a message. Here are the question numbers:*

10	7	1	4	9	2	6		11	3	8	5
		L									

The message is: ______________________!

2 Who says what?

▸ p. 11

a) Match the sentences to the speakers. Then check your answers on pp. 7–11 of your student's book.

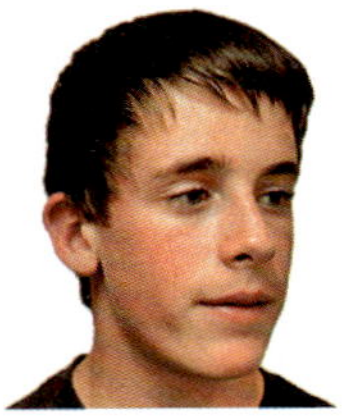

- I'm just a roadie for my brother's band.
- It's one of the Orkney Islands – north of Scotland.
- I'm a DJ.
- I love ice hockey.
- Oh, I'm mad about football.
- The islands are beautiful, but I'd really like to see London one day.
- I'll mail you some photos.
- We've got to keep in touch.
- Tell Hassan to come and do a gig in Manchester.

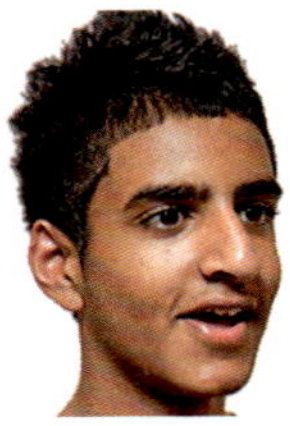

b) Write three sentences each about Asif, Katrina, Latisha and Robert.

Asif lives

Katrina comes

Latisha

Robert

3 WORDS Music words ▸ p. 11

a) *Find and write the music words in the list, then cross them out of the puzzle.*

~~b~~	~~a~~	~~n~~	~~d~~	s	~~k~~	e	~~y~~	~~b~~
~~o~~	~~a~~	~~r~~	~~d~~	p	c	o	n	c
e	r	t	o	c	l	a	r	i
n	e	t	g	i	g	o	f	l
u	t	e	a	t	r	u	m	p
e	t	c	h	o	i	r	n	d
r	u	m	s	e	v	i	o	l
i	n	h	g	u	i	t	a	r
r	e	c	o	r	d	e	r	x

band
keyboard
____
____
____
____
____
____
____
____
____
____

b) *Which letters are still in the puzzle? Put them in the correct order to make a new word for a musical instrument.*

0303 The instrument is: ____________________.

Now you

Write two paragraphs about music. How many different kinds of music do you know? What is your favourite kind of music? What kind of music don't you like? Would you like to go to a music festival? What do you think is good about music festivals? What do you think is maybe not so good? Read the picture story again on pp. 7–11 of your student's book for ideas.

0305

Revision

1 WORDS Lists ▸ p. 11

First find the group words or phrases. Write them at the top of the lists. Then write the words in the correct lists.

throat • valley • *places in town* • fields • shoulder • in the country • policeman • forest • *library* • department store • police station • hills • stomach • parts of the body • knee • photographer • post office • teacher • jobs • hospital • actor • lake • leg • leisure centre • engineer • village • head • shop assistant

1 *Places in town*	2	3	4
library			

0401

2 They all love music (Simple present: positive and negative sentences) ▸ p. 11

Complete with verbs in the simple present.

Robert *comes* (come) from Canada. Katrina, Latisha and Asif all *come* (come) from the UK, but they *don't know* (not know) anybody in Birmingham. When they ______ (meet) at the music festival, they soon ______ (become) good friends.

The four friends all ______ (love) music. Asif ______ (like) rap and Asian Fusion. Robert, Latisha and Katrina ______ (not know) anything about Asian Fusion, but Asif ______ (tell) them that it's a mixture of western and Asian music.

Asif ______ (not know) much about folk music, but Katrina ______ (love) it. She ______ (play) the fiddle in the school band and she ______ (practise) every day. Latisha's instrument is the steel drum, but she ______ (not practise) as often as Katrina. Robert and Asif ______ (not play) an instrument, but they both ______ (know) lots about music. They all ______ (think) the festival is great.

0503

3 Do they play an instrument? (Simple present: yes/no questions and short answers) ▸ p. 11

Hassan wants to know about Asif's new friends. Write his questions and Asif's answers.

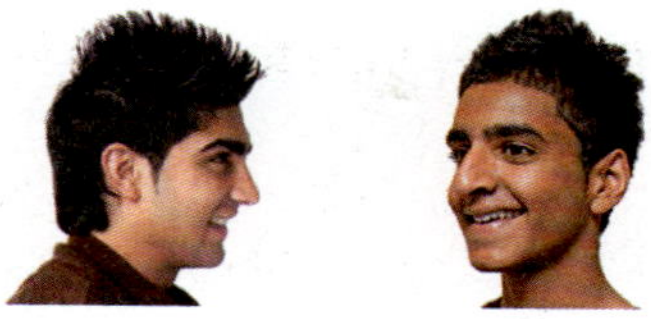

Hassan's questions: **Asif's answers:**

1 Robert – come from Canada?

Does Robert come from Canada? – Yes, he does.

2 Robert – play in a band?

______________________ – ______________

3 Katrina and Latisha – play an instrument?

______________________ – ______________

4 Latisha – come from the Orkneys?

______________________ – ______________

5 your friends – know what Asian Fusion is?

______________________ – ______________

6 they – want to come to our gig?

______________________ – ______________

0504 Great! Your new friends are cool!

4 Odd one out ▸ p. 11

Find the odd one out and write it down. Then write the letters. Put the letters in the right order and find the new word ▸.

1 rainy • foggy • stormy • noisily • cloudy — noisily (4) s

2 monkey • bear • lion • budgie • hippo — ______ (5) ___

3 skirt • shoulder • shirt • trousers • jacket — ______ (5) ___

4 river • sea • view • lake • pool — ______ (1) ___

5 engineer • painter • cooker • presenter • writer — ______ (5) ___

6 dishwasher • sink • cooker • washing machine • garage — ______ (2) ___

7 cool • great • wonderful • awful • fantastic — ______ (3) ___

8 pub • factory • town • station • cinema — ______ (1) ___

0402 ▸ The four friends meet at a ______________________ in Birmingham.

5 What are they doing? (Present progressive) ► p. 11

a) Write sentences in the present progressive.

1

2

3

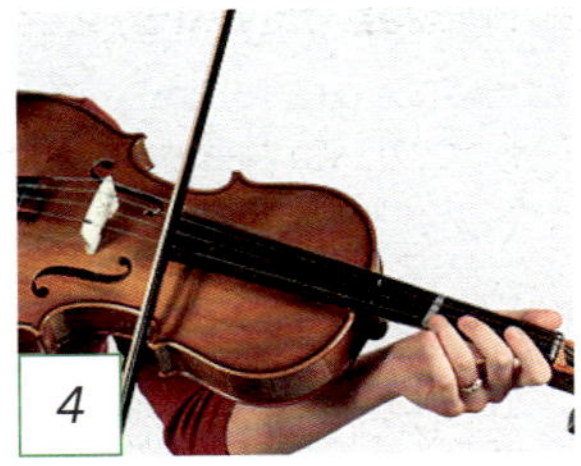
4

buy – tickets – workshop	chat – Katrina	have – snack	practise – fiddle

1 Just now the boys *are buying tickets for a workshop* ______.

2 At the moment Latisha ______.

3 Now Robert and Asif ______.

4 Just now Katrina ______.

b) Circle the correct form, simple present or present progressive.

1 Robert (doesn't like / isn't liking) waiting, but just now he ('s waiting / he waits) for Latisha and Katrina.

2 *Robert* Listen. Somebody (practises / is practising) the fiddle. Maybe it's Katrina.

She (practises / 's practising) every day. But Latisha (isn't practising / doesn't practise) every day. So where is she?

3 *Asif* Well, she (phones / 's phoning) her family every evening.

Maybe she (phones / 's phoning) now.

0605 Maybe she ('s telling / tells) everybody at home about our fantastic Asian Fusion band!

6 They went to Hassan's concert (Simple past: positive and negative statements) ► p. 11

Find the correct forms to complete the text.

answered • cheered • didn't get • didn't hear • didn't see • felt • found • had • looked • made • said • waved • *went* • were

Last night Robert and his new friends *went* to Hassan's gig. There ______ lots of people there.

Asif ______ to his brother excitedly, but Hassan ______ him.

Hassan ______ really cool on stage with his keyboard.

After the concert Hassan ______ Asif and the others. He ______, 'We ______ a few mistakes in the second song, didn't we?'

'Well, we ______ any mistakes,' Katrina ______.

'So you ______ it very wrong. Everybody ______ a fantastic time.

0606 And it ______ great when everybody ______ at the end. Really cool!'

7 After the festival (Simple past: questions and short answers)

▸ p. 11

Write questions about the music festival. Then write short answers.

1 Hassan **played** in a band. *Did* Katrina *play* in a band too? – Yes, *she did* .

2 Robert **stayed** with family in Birmingham. ___ the others ___ with family too? – No, ___ .

3 Katrina **slept** in the girls' hostel. ___ Latisha ___ there too? – Yes, ___ .

4 Latisha **played** the steel drum. ___ Katrina ___ the steel drum too? – ___ .

0707 5 Asif **went** to Hassan's gig. ___ Asif's friends ___ to the gig too? – ___ .

8 WORDS Pairs

▸ p. 11

Which words go together? Find and write pairs.

slow • rich • must • love • possible • strong • needn't • arrive • buy • closed • lose • hate • impossible • poor • *fast* • win • dirty • leave • weak • sad • sell • open • clean • happy

slow – *fast*   ___ – ___
___ – ___   ___ – ___
___ – ___   ___ – ___
___ – ___   ___ – ___
___ – ___   ___ – ___
0708 ___ – ___   ___ – ___

9 They've already packed their bags (Present perfect)

▸ p. 11

The music festival has finished. Write sentences about the four friends in the present perfect.

1

2

3

4

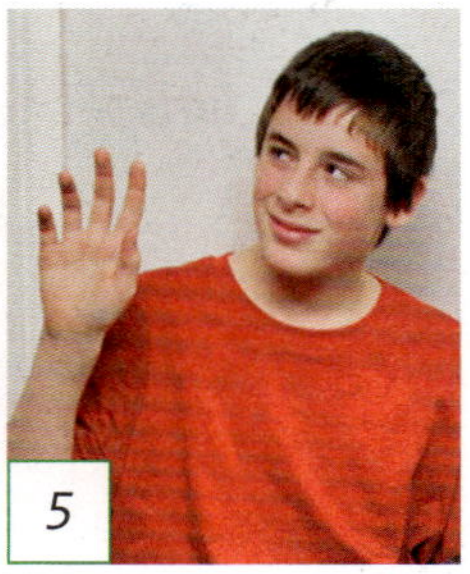
5

1 The friends *have already packed* their bags. (already, pack)

2 They ___ at the station. (just, arrive)

3 Katrina and Asif ___ some sandwiches to eat on the train. (buy)

4 Latisha's train to Manchester ___ . (already, leave)

0709 5 Robert ___ goodbye to Katrina and Asif. (just, say)

Unit 1 My London

1 London sights ▸ pp. 12–13

Match and write the sentences about the places 1–5 below. Before you start, write 1–5 after the sentences.

1 It's nice and green here. 3
2 It's on the river. ___
3 It's in the centre of town. ___
4 This is the best place to go if you like video games. ___
5 It's a famous market in east London. ___
6 It's free and you can look round all day. 4
7 On a clear day you can see for miles. ___
8 You can buy second-hand clothes and lots of cool stuff for young people here. ___
9 There are hundreds of games to choose from. ___
10 It isn't a cheap ride, but it's great. ___
11 You can see lots of famous old things, like very old locomotives and cars. ___
12 You can relax, walk or play ball games. ___
13 You can eat really interesting food here too. ___
14 They even play open-air concerts here. ___
15 If you like history and science, this is the place to go. ___

1 Brick Lane

___

___

2 The London Eye

___

3 Hyde Park

It's nice and green here.

4 The Science Museum

It's free and you can look round all day.

___

5 Funland, London Trocadero

___

___

0801

2 WORDS All about ... the London Underground ▸ p. 14

a) First, write the answers in the boxes.

1 Another word for the London Underground is ... 1

2 It's easier to find the way if you have a Tube ... 2

3 Sometimes you have to ... trains to a different line. 3

4 All the sights are in ... 1 and 2. 4

5 It's cheapest if you buy a ... 5

6 *Mrs Smith*: Which ... takes us to the London Eye? 6

7 *Robert*: First we take the ... Line to Bond Street. 7

8 *Mrs Smith*: Then we change to the Jubilee Line ... 8

9 *Robert*: And we get off the Tube at ... station. Easy! 9

0902
0903

b) Where does Asif like to go? Write the name of the place from the letters in the green boxes.

He likes to go to the ______________________.

3 LISTENING Going by Tube ▸ p. 14 2

Mark and his sister Mel are staying with their Uncle Dave in London. They're going to take the Tube and visit four sights. Listen carefully. Where do they want to go? Look at the map, then write down the names of the four Tube stations.

Info box

The Tube was the world's first underground. It started in 1863! About 3 million people ride on the Tube every day.

1 ______________________ 2 ______________________

3 ______________________ 4 ______________________

4 Word field: Transport ► p. 14, p. 20/P1, p. 173

Make a mind map for 'Transport' in your exercise book. You can use some of the words in the list more than once. You can add other words too. If some words are new, you can look at 'Word field: Transport' on p. 173.

airport • bike • boat • bus • bus pass • bus stop • cycle path • ferry • flight • gate • harbour • helicopter • line • northbound • plane • platform • railway • river • road • sea • ship • ticket • southbound • taxi • ticket machine • train • train station • tram • Travelcard • Tube • Tube station • tunnel

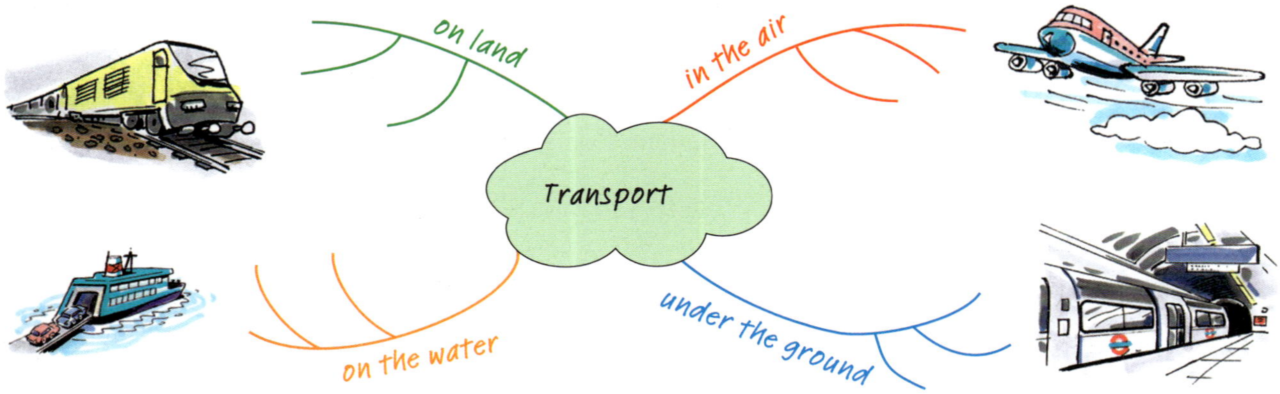

1004

Now you

Which is the best way to travel? What do you think, and why? Write six sentences or more in your exercise book.
Ideas: **safe**, **dangerous**, **fast**, **slow**, **interesting**, **boring**, **expensive**, **cheap**

5 PRONUNCIATION [aʊ] or [əʊ]? ► p. 15 3

Which words are like mouse *[aʊ] and which are like* mole *[əʊ]? Listen, say and match.*
Then write the words in two lists.

[aʊ]		[əʊ]	
cow		sofa	

1005

6 REVISION We had a great time (Simple past) ▸ p. 15 • GF 1a (p. 149)

Mel writes an e-mail to her best friend. Write the verbs in the simple past.

Hi from London!

It's fantastic here! Yesterday we *had* (have) a great day in town – and we *didn't get* (not get) lost[1]. We soon ______ (find) our way on the Tube, but we ______ (walk) for miles too. We ______ (visit) two of the biggest museums. We even ______ (see) 'The Gherkin'. We ______ (go) to Buckingham Palace, but we ______ (not do) the tour. So we ______ (not see) the Queen – ha ha! We ______ (buy) some postcards, but we ______ (not buy) any presents. Mark likes to take silly photos. Can you guess where he ______ (take) this one? Love, Mel

1106 I think Mark took this photo at ______.

7 REVISION The Feely family (Present perfect) ▸ p. 16 • GF 1b (p. 149)

Write about the Feely family. Choose the right reasons and the right adjectives from the boxes.

angry • excited • tired • ill • nervous • sad

eat lots of sweets • win some money • lose their kite • not sleep long enough • *kids – not clean room* • watch a scary DVD

1 Mrs Feely

2 Tommy Feely

3 Mo and Jo Feely

4 Grandpa Feely

5 Jill and Jenny

6 Mr Feely

1 *Mrs Feely is angry because the kids haven't cleaned their room.*

2 ______

3 ______

4 ______

5 ______

6 ______

[1] get lost *sich verlaufen*

8 STUDY SKILLS English–German dictionary ▸ p. 16 • SF (p. 135)

Read the text about Camden Market. Then answer the questions.

Camden Market draws tourists from all over the world. It is famous for its ethnic arts, crafts and second-hand clothes. You'll find textiles from the Middle East, hand-carved sculptures, Indian jewellery and lots more.
There are also exotic food stalls for delicious snacks, and there's a market hall for more exclusive things like antiques. Young people call Camden Market the hottest shopping and eating experience in London. But it is also a meeting place for artists, designers, film makers, pop and sports stars.
Visitors have called Camden Market 'the most interesting leisure village on the planet'.

1 *Try to understand the underlined words.*

I can guess these words from the context: ______________________________

These words are like German words: ______________________________

____

2 *Use an English–German dictionary to find the different meanings of these words. Then underline the right German meaning for the word in the text.*

draw: ______________________________

craft: ______________________________

experience: ______________________________

3 *Use an English–German dictionary to find and write the pronunciation of these words:*

jewellery [______________] antiques [______________] experience [______________]

9 What have they done? When did …? (Present perfect/Simple past) ▸ p. 16 • GF 1 (p. 149)

Underline the correct verb form. Present perfect or simple past?

1 Asif (has been/was) on the London Eye. He (was/has been) on it with Robert and his parents **yesterday**.

2 Robert (has tried/tried) Bangladeshi food. He (has tried/tried) it **when he was in Brick Lane with Asif**.

3 The Smiths (took/have taken) some great photos of London. They (took/have taken) them from the London Eye **yesterday**.

4 Mel (bought/has bought) some jeans at Brick Lane Market. She (bought/has bought) them **last Sunday**.

5 Mark (has played/ played) a virtual reality game at Funland. He (went/has gone) there **on Wednesday evening**.

1209 6 Mel and Mark (saw/have seen) 'The Lion King'. They (saw/have seen) it **last night** with their Uncle Dave.

10 Have you ever ...? (Present perfect/Simple past) ▸ p. 16 • GF 1 (p. 149)

Complete the dialogue with the present perfect or the simple past.

1 *Robert* ____________________ (you, ever, visit) the Science Museum?

2 *Asif* Oh, yes. I ____________ (see) Stephenson's Rocket a few times. It's really cool.

3 *Robert* When ____________ (go) there?

4 *Asif* Well, we ____________ (go) there with our form teacher about three years ago.

5 *Robert* London is so big. ____________________ (you, ever, get) lost?

6 *Asif* Oh, yes. I ____________ (get) lost in the museum on our school trip.

The teacher ____________ (not see) the famous rocket because

1310 he ____________ (have to) look for me!

11 WORDS Word building ▸ p. 17

a) *Which parts go together? Find and write the pairs. One word or two words?*

post	ticket	bus	cell	card	air	take	street	box	flea
phone	away	work	machine	market	shop	stop	port	performer	office

One word: postcard, ____________________

Two words: ticket machine, ____________________

b) *Now choose words from a) to complete the sentences.*

1 Brick Lane is a Sunday ____________ . You can buy everything from computers to sweets.

2 You can eat fantastic Bangladeshi food there too. There are lots of restaurants and ____________ .

3 Robert watched the ____________________ at Covent Garden. They were great.

4 The Smiths are taking the evening flight to Toronto, so they have to leave for the ____________ soon.

12 How long have you been in London? (Present perfect with since/for) ▸ p. 17 • GF 2 (p. 150)

An interviewer is asking tourists some questions. His first question is: 'How long have you been in London?' Complete what the people say with **since** *or* **for**.

We've been here since yesterday.

________ my birthday last week.

We've been here ________ a week.

________ about ten days now.

________ last Friday, I think.

1312

I've been here ________ ten years – I live here!

Now you

*How long have you done these things? In your exercise book, write two sentences with **since** and two with **for**:*

1 lived in your village, town or city
2 been in your new school class
3 known your English teacher
4 had your pet, bike or computer

I've/We've lived in our town for about five years. Or: *I've/We've lived in our town since 2003.*

13 London scenes (Present perfect progressive with since/for)

▸ p. 17 • GF 2 (p. 150)

*Make a sentence for each photo. Use the present perfect progressive with **since** or **for**.*

1 wait – next Tube – five minutes

2 choose postcards – ten minutes

3 sit – Hyde Park – 10 o'clock

4 listen to – rock band – half an hour

5 run – Regent's[1] Park – 9.30

6 feed the birds – in Regent's Park – breakfast

7 look round – museum – over an hour

1 The people *have been waiting for the next Tube for five minutes.*
2 The woman ______________________.
3 These people ______________________.
4 They ______________________.
5 This man ______________________.
6 The man ______________________.
1413 7 These people ______________________.

Now you

*How long have you been doing these things? In your exercise book, write two sentences with **for** and two with **since**:*

1 learning English
2 using the internet
3 playing computer or video games
4 doing your homework today

[1] Regent's [ri'dʒənts]

14 WRITING COURSE Part 1: Writing better sentences (An e-mail)

▸ *p. 17, p. 24/P 11 • SF (p. 146)*

a) *How can you make your sentences better? Tick (✓) four boxes.*

- use more adjectives, like *great, interesting* ☐
- use very short sentences ☐
- use adverbs like *very, really, usually* ☐
- use time phrases like *every day, now* ☐
- use linking words like *and, but, so, because* ☐
- start every sentence with *I, We* or *It* ☐

b) *Mark examples of adjectives, adverbs, time phrases and linking words on the two e-mails. Which one is more interesting, Ben's e-mail or Sam's e-mail? Why?*

1

Dear Asif

We're in Wales. It's nice here. It has rained a bit. It's sunny too. We're in a B&B. The breakfast is good. My room is small. We went to a castle. It was nice. We're going to visit a museum too.

Love, Ben

2

Dear Asif

We're in Wales and we're having a great time. On Monday it rained so we went shopping, but now it's warm and sunny. We're staying at a very nice B&B. My room is a bit small, but breakfast is fantastic. The people are friendly too. We usually walk on the beach in the mornings. Yesterday we visited Cardiff Castle - really interesting. We're going to visit a famous museum tomorrow.

Love, Sam

I think ____________ is more interesting than ____________ because ____________

more ____.

c) *You are on holiday in London. Write an e-mail to a friend in Germany. Say where you are, what the weather is like, what you did yesterday, what you are going to do tomorrow. Use the more interesting e-mail in b) for ideas.*

Dear ____

Fun fact

In London there are more than 6000 restaurants, 5000 pubs, 100 theatres – and 300 different languages!

15 Extra Background File LONDON ▸ pp. 18–19

a) *Read pp. 18–19 in your student's book again. Then match the pictures to the 7 steps.*

Step *1* ☐ Step *2* ☐ Step *3* ☐ Step *4* ☐ Step *5* ☐ Step *6* ☐ Step *7* ☐

b) *Right or wrong? Tick (✓) the correct letter and write it down in c).*

		Right	Wrong
1	You won't find cheap clothes at Covent Garden or Camden Lock.	P	L
2	You can find trendy clothes by young designers at some of the London markets.	E	I
3	You can see some of the most famous paintings in the world in the National Gallery.	I	C
4	You can only use your Travelcards before 9.30.	E	C
5	The Docklands Light Railway goes past the skyscrapers of the City of London.	E	A
6	At the Natural History Museum you can see lots of old pictures.	D	S
7	There are lots of homeless people on the streets of London.	T	I
8	People in London like to eat lamb biryani for lunch, often in one of the parks.	L	E
9	You can find Nelson's Column in Trafalgar Square.	R	L

c) *If all your answers are correct, you have written the name of another famous square in London.*

The name is: ___ ___ ___ ___ ___ ___ ___ ___ ___ Square

How do you say the name? Look on p. 171 of your student's book for the answer.

d) *Complete the text with these words:* culture • designer • on a budget • second-hand • skyscrapers • free

London has something for everybody, even for kids ____________ . For example, you can buy cool ____________ clothes at some of London's markets – even young ____________ clothes. If you have time for a bit of ____________ , the best museums are ____________ . When you have seen the famous old buildings, you can use your Travelcard to see London's fantastic ____________ from the DLR. For lunch you can eat a sandwich in one of the many parks. And remember, if you need ideas for a London project, lots of tourist information is free too.

16 Blue box: Buildings and places in a town

▸ p. 19, p. 171

What can you see in Mark's photos? Look carefully at the pictures of London in your student's book. Then match and write the names.

Nelson's	Lane
St Paul's	Column
Buckingham	Square
Brick	Lock
Piccadilly	Palace
Trafalgar	Cathedral
Camden	Bridge
Tower	Circus

1

Nelson's Column

2

3

4

5

17 EVERYDAY ENGLISH Asking for and giving information

▸ p. 19, p. 25/P 13

Look at the picture. What do you think ***A*** *(Frau) and* ***B*** *(Frau am Schalter) are saying?*
Write a short dialogue in your exercise book. Use ideas from the box:

Can I help you? • How long ...? • How much is ...? • Where ...? • under 16 • 7 pounds 50 • about an hour • Thank you. • You're welcome.

18 WORKING WITH THE TEXT Only a game

▸ pp. 26–28

a) *Read pp. 26–28 of your student's book again. Who said what? Tick (✔) the correct box.*

1	They've got over 250 video games.	☐	☐
2	Sounds cool. Let's try one.	☐	☐
3	Look, we can choose a virtual world.	☐	☐
4	This is getting too realistic for me.	☐	☐
5	It's only a game.	☐	☐
6	It's him. It's Jack the Ripper.	☐	☐
7	I don't want to die!	☐	☐

b) *Match the parts to make true sentences.*

1	When Robert and Asif arrived at the Trocadero,	he didn't really want to play the game.
2	Robert didn't know how virtual reality games worked,	Robert did what Asif told him.
3	When Robert read the words 'Play at your own risk',	a woman's voice told them to stop.
4	When Asif said 'Push the button',	so Asif explained it to him.
5	When the boys made a joke about Jack the Ripper,	they went to Funland.
6	As they were walking in the foggy streets,	the boys thought it was Jack the Ripper.
7	When they took the helmets off,	Asif felt a rat run over his foot.
8	When a long shadow appeared,	nothing happened.
9	When the angry people on the street saw the boys,	they thought they were murderers.

c) *At the beginning of the visit to Funland, Robert is* ***more careful*** *and* ***more scared*** *than Asif. Read ll. 1–100 again. Find and write down three sentences or more that show us this. Write the number of the lines in the text too.*

____

____

____

____

____

d) *Do you think the story so far is exciting, scary, boring, silly or unrealistic? Write four or more sentences in your exercise book.*

I think the story so far is ...

1 Transport: What is it?

1 a ______________

2 ______________

3 ______________

4 ______________

5 ______________

6 ______________

1901

2 Have you ever ...?

Make sentences with the verb in the present perfect or simple past.

Asif ______________ (you, ever, eat) anything strange?

Robert You mean like real *English* food? Yes, I have. I ______________ (eat) fish and chips last week. Joke! Sorry! ______________ (you, ever, try) our food?

Asif You mean hamburgers and chips? Joke! Sorry! Has Canada got a national dish?

Robert They eat yellow pea[1] soup in the French part of Canada. I ______________ (eat) that lots of times.

Asif Sounds good. I love soup. When ______________ (you, have) it the last time?

1902 *Robert* We ______________ (have) it on my grandpa's birthday in Quebec[2] last December.

3 Since or for?

1 Asif has lived in the East End ______________ ten years.

2 Asif and Robert have been eating in a Bangladeshi restaurant ______________ 1 o'clock.

1903 *3* They have been talking about video games and Funland ______________ at least an hour.

4 Underline the correct verb form.

1 We've (been knowing/known) our English teacher for two years.

2 Since their trip on the Eye, the Smiths (have been walking/have walked) around London.

1904 *3* Robert (has had/has been having) a new computer since Christmas last year.

18 points

Now you

Imagine you were in London with your family for two days. Write an e-mail about it to an English friend. Say what you did, where you went, what you saw, what you ate, what you liked best. You can use the information in your student's book. Write eight sentences or more in your exercise book. Use paragraphs and topic sentences.

1905
1906 *We have just come back from a short holiday in England. We were in London for two days ...*

[1] pea [piː] *Erbse* [2] Quebec [kwɪ'bek] *Stadt in Kanada*

Unit 2 Island girl

1 About Hoy ▸ pp. 30–31

a) *Look at pp. 30–31 of your student's book again. Then read the sentences and tick (✔) the right letter in the 'right' or 'wrong' boxes. Write the letters below ▸.*

	Right	Wrong
1 The Orkney Islands are in the North Sea.	K✓	L
2 Hoy is bigger than the Mainland.	I	A
3 The Old Man of Hoy is the oldest man on the island.	I	T
4 In the green fields of Hoy you can see lots of sheep and cows.	R	S
5 There are a few shops on Hoy.	H	I
6 A salmon farmer's job is hard work.	N	A
7 Hoy has a big oil terminal.	E	A

If your answers are correct, you have written the name of somebody who lives on Hoy.

▸ The person is K ________________________.

b) *Write these 'Orkney words' correctly.*

ldinass	phese	lishl	mlnaos merfars	cynesre
islands				

c) *Choose two photos of Hoy (photos B, D, E or F) from pp. 30–31 of your student's book. Describe the photos in a paragraph each. Use* **on the right/left, in the foreground/background/middle, at the top, at the bottom.** *Read your description out in class. The class must guess the photo.*

____

____

____

____

____

____

____

____

____

____

____

2002

2 Word field: Town and country ► p. 31, p. 38/P1, p. 178

a) Some letters are missing in the town and country words. First, fill in the missing letters.

Town and city words		Country words	
poli__e sta__ion	a_i_rpo_r_t	f____lds	s__enery
tr____fic	mos__ue	__anal	for__st
t__eat____	cathedr__l	v__lley	h__lls
synagog____	under__ro__nd	ba_y_	m____ntains
shopping pr____inct	depar__ment stor__	coa____	se__

b) Now write the word lists in alphabetical order.

Town words: airport, ______

______

2102 **Country words:** bay, ______

______

3 WORDS All about ... electronic media ► p. 32

Find and write 'electronic media' words.

m	o	b	i	l	e	d	m	t
e	g	m	n	o	u	o	c	e
s	c	j	t	g	c	w	l	x
s	s	e	e	o	h	n	d	t
a	s	u	r	f	a	l	w	k
g	r	i	n	g	t	o	n	e
e	l	s	e	n	d	a	s	h
k	p	v	t	v	i	d	e	o
p	e	-	m	a	i	l	h	r

2103

►	▼
mobile	message
______	______
______	______
______	______
______	______
______	______

Fun fact
In December 2006 for the first time there were more mobiles in Germany than people!

Now you

What do you think these text messages mean?

1 C u 2nite — See you tonight.
2 R u ok? ______
3 U r gr8 ______
4 C u l8er ______
5 Fone 2mw pls ______
6 Wot r u doin 2mw? ______
______

4 PRONUNCIATION Stress in words with three or more syllables ▸ p. 32 🎧 4

a) *How do you say these words? Is the stress on the first, second or third syllable? Say the words, mark the stress and write 1, 2 or 3 in the box. Then listen to the words and check your answers.*

1 acrobat	1	6 dishwasher	___	11 explorer	___
2 allergic	___	7 documentary	___	12 mediation	___
3 announcement	___	8 electricity	___	13 realistic	___
4 biology	___	9 elevator	___	14 recording	___
5 description	___	10 engineer	___	15 scenery	___

b) *Write three more 'long' words each. You can use the Dictionary in your student's book.*

1 Words with the stress on the **first** syllable: ____________________

2 Words with the stress on the **second** syllable: ____________________

2204 3 Words with the stress on the **third** syllable: ____________________

5 The Feely family (Present progressive with future meaning) ▸ p. 33 • GF 4c (p. 152)

What are the Feelys doing next week? Use these words:

play the trumpet/school concert • paint/kitchen • watch/football match/TV • clean/car • go/art class • have/party

1 Mrs Feely

2 Grandpa Feely

3 Mo and Jo

4 Tommy Feely

5 Jill and Jenny

6 Mr Feely

1 On Monday Mrs Feely is going to her art class.

2 On Tuesday ____________________.

3 On Wednesday ____________________.

4 On Thursday ____________________.

5 On Friday ____________________.

2205 6 On Saturday ____________________.

6 WRITING COURSE Part 2: Using paragraphs (Describing what happened)

▸ p. 33, p. 39/P4 • SF (p. 146)

a) Here's an e-mail from Katrina to Latisha. Put the parts in the correct order. Write the numbers 1–5 in the boxes.

Well, first Morag wanted to show me the city sights. We didn't take the bus tour – we walked everywhere! Edinburgh Castle was so cool. It stands on a hill, so we had to walk up to the top. We did the tour and I took some really cool photos. ☐

Must stop now and do my French homework – yuck! I hope you like the photos.
Write soon and tell me what's happening in exciting Manchester!
Love, Kat ☐

Before we went home, I found a fantastic shop for musical instruments, trumpets, guitars – and fiddles, of course. We spent half an hour in the shop – poor Morag. But we had lots of fun and it was a great day. We were at home at 6, then Morag's friends came. ☐

Hi Tish!
Guess where I was last weekend! I went to visit my favourite cousin in Edinburgh. It was her birthday. Edinburgh is a great city, so I'll tell you all about it. ☐

At lunchtime we went to Morag's favourite café. We had soup and sandwiches. They had great strawberry smoothies too. Then we walked up the Royal Mile and Princes Street – great shops. We went into a big CD shop and chose Morag's birthday present together – a cool CD of her favourite band. ☐

b) How do you write an interesting e-mail? Find and write an example of these things in Katrina's e-mail:

1 Make your opening sentence interesting.

Guess where I was last weekend!

2 At the beginning say what your e-mail is about.

____

3 Start a new paragraph for each new idea. Use First ..., At lunchtime ..., etc. *(Write three topic sentences).*

a ______________________________

b ______________________________

c ______________________________

4 Finish with something personal.

____

c) In your exercise book, write an e-mail to a new friend. Tell him/her about a really good day with family or friends, or about a class trip. Give your e-mail a structure. You can use Katrina's e-mail as an example.

7 WORDS The prefix un- (Word formation) ▸ p. 33

a) *Complete the list.*

able	–	*unable*
clear	–	______
comfortable	–	______
cool	–	______
friendly	–	______
interesting	–	______
safe	–	______
true	–	______

b) *Now choose words with the prefix* **un-** *from a) and complete the sentences.*

1 'Is it *unsafe* ______ to go by ferry in a storm, Katrina?'

2 'Not always. When there's a storm, the journey is ______.'

3 It's ______ to be ______ to your classmates or to bully them.

2407 4 There are lots of stories about scary things in Scottish castles, but most of them are ______.

8 I'll answer it (will-future, spontaneous decisions) ▸ p. 34 • GF 5 (p. 153)

Look at the pictures. What do you think Katrina will say? Use the words under the pictures and **will** *or* **won't**.

answer

I'll answer it. ______

______

help

Just a minute. ______

______

tell – Mum

Don't worry, Dad! ______

______

go to the shop

No problem. ______

______

look for

No, I'm busy. ______

______

meet – in ten minutes

OK. ______

______

Just for fun

2408

9 REVISION If she doesn't get up, … (Conditional sentences 1) ▸ p. 34 • GF 6a (p. 153)

*It's Monday morning. Katrina has to get up, but she's still tired. What will happen if she doesn't get up soon? Write sentences with **If …** and **will/won't**.*

1 not get up soon – leave home too late
2 leave home too late – miss the ferry
3 miss the ferry – not get the school bus
4 not get the school bus – be too late for lessons on Monday
5 take the next ferry – not get to school till 4 pm

1 *If she doesn't get up soon, she'll leave home too late.*

2 ______________________________

3 ______________________________

4 ______________________________

2509 5 ______________________________

10 LISTENING If we went to Majorca, … ▸ p. 35 🎧 5

Mr and Mrs Preston and the kids, Leo and Marie, are talking about their next family holiday. Listen carefully and choose the correct answer, A, B or C.

1 Who would like to go on holiday on the Scottish islands?
A Mr Preston. B Mrs Preston. C Marie.

2 Mr Preston would like a holiday in the country because … A he could go for long walks.
B he could go swimming in the sea. C he could watch the animals and the birds.

3 Leo thinks a holiday on a Scottish island would be … A exciting. B boring. C healthy.

4 Mr Preston doesn't want to go to Majorca because … (two answers are correct)
A it's too noisy. B there are too many people. C it's too hot.

5 Mr Preston would like to go to France because … A he wants to speak French.
B he thinks Leo and Marie could practise their French. C he likes the food.

6 If the family went somewhere exciting, Leo and Marie … A would have to speak French.
B wouldn't make new friends. C could do a great school project.

7 If they went to Scotland, …
A Marie and Leo would make lots of new friends. B the weather would be good.
C it would be cheaper.

11 If I lived like Robinson Crusoe, … (Conditional sentences 2) ▸ p. 35 • GF 6 (pp. 153–154)

a) *What do you think Leo is thinking?*
Look at the pictures and finish the sentences.

1 **play football – monkeys**

If I lived like Robinson Crusoe, *I would play football with the monkeys.*

1

2 **build**

3 **catch**

4 **sleep – treehouse**

5 **go swimming – dolphins**[1]

2 If I lived like Robinson Crusoe, I would ______________________.

3 If I had nothing to eat, ______________________.

4 If I was afraid of wild animals, ______________________.

5 If I had nothing to do, ______________________.

b) *If Leo lived like Robinson Crusoe, what* **wouldn't** *he do? Complete the sentences with the correct forms of the verbs in brackets.*

1 If Leo *lived* (live) like Robinson Crusoe, he *wouldn't go* (not go) to school.

2 If he *didn't go* (not go) to school, he ______________ (not do) homework.

3 If he ______________ (not do) homework, he ______________ (not learn) anything.

4 If he ______________ (not learn) anything, he ______________ (not get) a job.

2611 5 But he ______________ (not need) a job if he ______________ (live) like Robinson Crusoe!

12 If … (Conditional sentences 2) ▸ p. 35 • GF 6 (pp. 153–154)

Imagine these situations and complete the sentences.

1 If I found fifty euros on the street, *I'd (probably) tell my parents/feel happy.*

2 If my mum or dad won lots of money, they ______________________.

3 If there was a bully in our class, we ______________________.

4 If I heard strange noises in the night, I ______________________.

5 If we moved to a new town, I ______________________.

2612 6 If we didn't do our homework, our English teacher ______________________.

[1] dolphin ['dɒlfɪn] *Delfin*

13 It would be fantastic if, … (Conditional sentences 2)

▸ p. 35 • GF 6 (pp. 153–154)

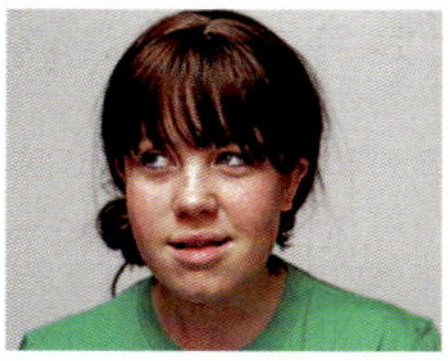

What do you think Katrina is thinking? Use the words to complete the sentences.

1 Latisha – come to visit me on Hoy

'I would be very excited if ______________________.'

2 the Beauties – always – call me Fishface

'It would be awful if ______________________.'

3 the Beauties – be as nice as Latisha

2713

'It would be great if ______________________.'

Just for fun

Boy I'm late for football practice. Dad, could you do my Maths homework for me?

Dad But son, if I did your Maths homework, it wouldn't be right.

Boy Well, a few wrong answers are OK, Dad. Just do your best.

Now you

If you lived on Hoy, how would your life be different? What would you do?
What wouldn't you do? Write two paragraphs in your exercise book. Begin each paragraph with a topic sentence.
If I lived on Hoy like Katrina, my life would be very different. I would have to go to school by …

14 STUDY SKILLS Using a German–English dictionary

▸ p. 35 • SF (pp. 136)

You have an English friend. He/She is unhappy at school because some students bully him/her. You write this e-mail to your friend. Use a German–English dictionary to find the words in brackets. Write down all the English translations. Then mark the correct one and write it next to the e-mail.

Hi …!
I hope this mail will (1 dich aufmuntern).
The bullies are (2 bloß) jealous[1]. You play the violin really well – and they can only play CDs! So they (3 machen sich über dich lustig) because it makes them feel good. It (4 erinnert mich) of the time when some classmates bullied me because I wore glasses. The (5 Grund) was, I was much better at sport and Maths than they were! The bullies have problems – not you! Take my advice, don't think about them.
Tell your friends, your parents or your teacher. Nobody likes bullies.
But lots of people like you!

Correct

1 *cheer you up*
2 ______
3 ______
4 ______
5 ______

1 ***aufmuntern***: *1(ermuntern) encourage; 2(aufheitern) cheer up*

2 ***bloß***: ______________________

3 ***lustig***: ______________________

4 ***erinnern***: ______________________

5 ***Grund***: ______________________

[1] jealous ['dʒeləs] *eifersüchtig, neidisch*

15 MEDIATION Loch Ness and Nessie ▸ p. 35 • SF (p. 143)

You read this article about the Loch Ness Monster. Tell a German friend the most important facts in a few German sentences. Mark key sentences or words and make notes. Write in your exercise book.

Over the last 14 centuries, over ten thousand people have said that they have seen the Loch Ness Monster – but was it Nessie? There is no proof that there really is a monster in the lake.
People don't agree what Nessie looks like. Reports and photos are always different. Some have said that Nessie looks like half a horse and half a snake, with a long neck[1] like a giraffe. One person said the monster looked like a kind of dinosaur or a swimming elephant.
In May 2007, 55-year-old Gordon Holmes from the north of England even took a video of something in Loch Ness. People all over the world watched it on TV. Mr Holmes described the monster as 'a jet black[2] thing about 45 feet long, moving fast in the water'.
If there is a Nessie, it probably lives about 300 metres down – in the coldest part of the lake. And because it doesn't come to the top very often, it's probably quite shy ...

Info box

Scotland has 787 islands, but people live on only 120 of them.

16 WORDS Verbs and nouns (Word formation) ▸ p. 35

a) *Sometimes you have the same form for verbs and nouns: (to) **phone**, **the phone**. And sometimes there are different forms: (to) **argue**, **the argument**. Complete the table.*

VERB	NOUN	VERB	NOUN
answer	*answer*	rehearse	
build			smell
describe		smile	
feel			start
	flight		surprise
laugh		survive	
	listener		translation
mean		visit	

b) *Now complete the sentences with words from the table.*

1 How do you ______ 'gemein' into English? Who knows the ______?

2 I don't know the ______ of this German word. What does it ______?

3 Katrina often ______ upset. It isn't a nice ______ to be called 'Fishface'.

4 When the teacher isn't in the classroom, the Beauties ______ about Katrina's clothes and hair. But when the teacher comes in, the ______ stops.

2816

[1] neck [nek] *Hals* [2] jet black [dʒet 'blæk] *pechschwarz*

17 Extra Background File Scotland quiz

▸ pp. 36–37

a) Choose the correct answer, A, B or C. You need the letters in brackets in b).

1 Ben Nevis is ...

A a Scottish singer. (G)	B a mountain. (E)	C a Scottish actor. (I)

2 'Clan' means ...

A club. (B)	B area. (A)	C family. (E)

3 'Gaelic' is ...

A a national dish. (T)	B a language. (R)	C one of the Orkney Islands. (G)

4 'Haggis' is ...

A something to wear. (S)	B a festival. (L)	C something to eat. (E)

5 A 'kilt' is a kind of ...

A skirt. (A)	B trousers. (D)	C shirt. (E)

6 Alexander Fleming was ...

A an actor. (B)	B a famous writer. (E)	C a doctor and scientist. (N)

7 The traditional musical instrument of Scotland is ...

A the trumpet. (S)	B the bagpipes. (D)	C the saxophone. (A)

8 'Shortbread' is a kind of ...

A cake. (G)	B bread. (D)	C biscuit. (B)

b) Now write the letters next to your answers in the boxes. If your answers are correct, the letters make the name of another city in Scotland. Here are the question numbers:

5	8	2	3	7	1	4	6
					E		

c) Write what you know about the city in b) from your student's book, pp. 36–37. Find more interesting facts on the internet and write a paragraph. Remember to begin with a topic sentence.

18 WORKING WITH THE TEXT Orkney Star ▸ pp. 45–48

a) Read pp. 45–48 in your student's book again. Who probably thought what? Match the bubbles to the people.

What a terrible surprise! I can't believe that Fishface will be the star of the film!

Katrina is nicer than Fiona and the others. I wonder if she'll notice my ponytail ...

Ah! Katrina wears wellies and a ponytail – just like me.

I hope they will enjoy my stew. Maybe they've never eaten an Orkney dish before.

I'm not ready and I'm nervous. I hope I don't say anything silly.

b) When did the people in a) probably think these things? Complete the sentences with **when** *... , or* **just before** *...*

1 Fiona probably thought this *when she heard the head teacher's announcement about Katrina.*

2 Katrina probably thought this *just before* ______________________.

3 Katrina's mum ______________________.

4 Sheena ______________________.

5 Alison ______________________.

c) Imagine you are Katrina. In your exercise book, write an e-mail to Latisha about your week with the film crew.

Hi Tish!

I've had a fantastic week! Let me tell you about it!

...

Write soon!

Love, Katrina

19 Blue box: to the doctor's ... ▸ p. 48, p. 179

Complete what Katrina's parents say with: to the hairdresser's | from the chemist's | to the doctor's

Dad I don't feel well today. It's my stomach. I think I'll go ______________________.

Mum I'm going to Kirkwall ______________________ today. Maybe I can get you something for your stomach ______________________. Then you can stay at home and watch TV all day.

Dad Good idea!

1 Town and country: Write the words.

1 c______________

2 s________p______

3 ______________n

4 ______________y

5 c________p______

6 s______________y

3101

2 If I had more pocket money, …

Complete the dialogue with the correct verb forms.

Leo My friends get more pocket money than me.
If I ______________ (have) more, …

Marie … you ______________ (spend) more on silly things.

Leo That isn't true. If I ______________ (get) five pounds more, I ______________ (save) it for a new MP3 player.

Marie If I ______________ (want) more money, I ______________ (find) a Saturday job.

3102 *Leo* No, not a good idea. If I ______________ (work) on Saturdays,
I ______________ (have to) get up before lunchtime.

3 Computers and mobiles

Complete with 'electronic media' words.

Leo likes to ______________ to his friends on his computer after school. It's cheaper than phone calls. He likes to ______________ the internet too. It's more fun than homework. Marie likes to send ______________ messages to her friends on her mobile. She thinks it's more fun than ______________ messages on the computer. She has a cool ______________ on her mobile, a picture of her cat, Tabby. And guess what her ______________ is – Tabby too!
3103 When her phone rings on the bus, everybody looks for a cat!

20 points

Now you

If you went on holiday to Scotland, what would you like to see or do? Write two or three paragraphs in your exercise book. Remember to use topic sentences. Ideas: Orkney Islands, Edinburgh, Loch Ness Monster.

3104
3105 *I think Scotland must be a very nice place for a holiday. If we went to Scotland, I'd like to visit the Orkney Islands …*

Here are some exercises that will help you with your practice test 1.

1 WORDS A day in the country (Prepositions) ▸ pp. 50–51

Underline the correct preposition.

For my art teacher I had to paint a picture (of /from) a country scene. ‘We can go (for/on) a walk (to/till) the old farmhouse (by/on) the river. Or we can go (by/with) bike. You can walk (up/to) the hill and paint your scene from there, Jimmy,’ said Mum.

Dad listened (to/at) the weather report (in/on) the radio, and there were only a few white clouds (in/on) the sky, so we went (on/by) foot.

(At/On) the top of the hill there was a good view (of/from) the area. I painted my picture. (On/At) the right I painted the farmhouse, with a horse (on/in) the yard. (Between/Round) the farmhouse and the river there were some cows (in/on) a field. There was a village (on/at) the left and hills and woods (in/at) the background. I was proud (of/for) my picture. Fantastic!

But then it suddenly started to rain – (on/over) my picture too. Oh, no! It looked awful. I was afraid (of/for) what Mr Wilson, my art teacher, would say …

(On/At) Monday afternoon (in/at) the art lesson Mr Wilson said, ‘This is a very modern water colour, Jimmy. Well done!’

2 What are they doing? (Present progressive) ▸ pp. 50–51

Describe what the people in the picture are doing. Complete the sentences with the present progressive of a verb from the box.

fly • have • read • sit • swim • take

1 A little *boy is flying a kite.*

2 Two girls ______________________.

3 A man ______________________.

4 Two boys ______________________.

5 Four people ______________________.

6 A girl ______________________.

3 Yesterday (Simple past)

▸ pp. 50–51 Irregular verbs (pp. 245–246)

Write the simple past forms, then write a short sentence with three verbs. Begin with 'Yesterday ...'

Infinitive:	go	buy	lose	find	make	see
Simple past:	*went*	______	______	______	______	______

Yesterday I went to town. Yesterday ________________________________

____

____

4 Spelling (Same sound, different words)

▸ pp. 50–51

The words sound the same but the spelling is different. Complete with the correct word.

1 road, rode

He ____________ his bike up the ____________ to school.

2 role, roll

I've got a ____________ in the school play.

For breakfast I usually have cornflakes, then a ____________ or toast.

3 who's, whose

Do you know ____________ book this is?

Do you know ____________ coming to the party tomorrow?

4 through, threw

I ____________ the ball to my friend, but it went ____________ a neighbour's window.

5 WRITING Writing better sentences

▸ pp. 50–51 • SF (p. 146)

The text below is boring. Write it again. Add words and phrases from the green box to make it more interesting.

after a few minutes • almost • loud • loudly • on the lake • really • so • soon • strange • strong • suddenly • then • under the trees • very • *yesterday*

... it was a hot day ... I went to the park lake. / I sat down ... and ... I was asleep. / I had a ... dream. / I was in a boat .../ It was dark and ... quiet. / ... I found that the boat had a hole. / ... it was ... full of water. / I felt ...scared. / ... I heard a ... voice. / Somebody shouted my name ... / A ... hand grabbed my arm. 'Here you are, asleep!' said Dad.

Yesterday ________________________________

____

____

____

____

____

Jetzt kann ich ...	Sehr gut!	OK	Verbessern!
HÖREN: Ich kann ...			
... eine längere Geschichte verstehen, auch wenn mir einige Wörter nicht bekannt sind.	☐	☐	☐
... aus Listening-Übungen Details richtig entnehmen.	☐	☐	☐
... den schottischen Akzent sowie ein paar schottische Wörter (z.B. *ceilidh*) erkennen und verstehen.	☐	☐	☐
... die Wörter der Units 1 und 2 verstehen.	☐	☐	☐
SPRECHEN: Ich kann ...			
... meine Meinung zu Themen im Englischunterricht frei äußern, auch wenn ich Fehler mache.	☐	☐	☐
... nach dem Weg fragen und anderen den Weg erklären.	☐	☐	☐
... über elektronische Medien sprechen.	☐	☐	☐
... die Laute [*now* : aʊ] und [*no:* əʊ] voneinander unterscheiden und richtig aussprechen.	☐	☐	☐
... Wörter mit drei und mehr Silben richtig betonen, auch wenn die Betonung im Deutschen anders ist (z.B. *'instrument, presen'tation*).	☐	☐	☐
... die Wörter der Units 1 und 2 richtig aussprechen und anwenden.	☐	☐	☐
LESEN: Ich kann ...			
... die längeren Texte und Dialoge der Units 1 und 2 lesen und verstehen.	☐	☐	☐
... die längeren Texte und Dialoge der Units 1 und 2 ohne Probleme laut lesen.	☐	☐	☐
... Texte über Themen des Alltags lesen und verstehen, auch wenn mir einige Wörter nicht bekannt sind.	☐	☐	☐
SCHREIBEN: Ich kann ...			
... kurze Texte (E-Mail, Postkarte) schreiben.	☐	☐	☐
... einfache Fragen zu Texten der Units 1 und 2 schriftlich beantworten.	☐	☐	☐
... meine Sätze mit *adjectives, adverbs, time phrases* und *linking words* verbinden und ausbauen, um sie sprachlich interessanter zu gestalten.	☐	☐	☐
... meine Texte in *beginning, middle* und *end* sinnvoll unterteilen.	☐	☐	☐
... meine Absätze mit *topic sentences* einleiten und jeden neuen Aspekt mit einem neuen Absatz anfangen.	☐	☐	☐
LAND UND LEUTE: Ich ...			
... kenne die Namen einiger berühmten Sehenswürdigkeiten in London (z.B. *Buckingham Palace, the London Eye, the Gherkin, St Paul's Cathedral*).	☐	☐	☐
... könnte mich im Londoner *Tube*-Netz zurechtfinden. Mehrere Namen der *Tube stations* und *lines* sind mir geläufig (z.B. *Queensway, Waterloo, Bond Street, Central Line, Jubilee Line*).	☐	☐	☐
... weiß, dass in London viele ethnische Gruppen leben.	☐	☐	☐
... habe einiges über Schottland, die schottischen Inseln und über die schottische Sprache gelernt.	☐	☐	☐

Jetzt kann ich ...

	Sehr gut!	OK	Verbessern!
GRAMMATIKVERSTÄNDNIS: Ich kann ...			
... das Futur mit *will* für spontane Entschlüsse (bei einem Hilfsangebot oder Versprechen) richtig verwenden (z.B. *I'll help you with your bags/ I won't forget to phone you tonight*).	☐	☐	☐
... mit dem *present progressive* über feste Pläne und Verabredungen in der Zukunft sprechen, auch 'Kalender-Zukunft' genannt (z.B. *On Friday after school I'm meeting some friends in town*).	☐	☐	☐
... mit einem *Conditional sentence* (*type* 2) ausdrücken, was unter bestimmten Bedingungen geschehen wäre oder nicht. Dazu benutze ich im *if*-Satz das *simple past* und im Hauptsatz *would/could/might* + Infinitiv (z.B. *If I lived in London, I would have an exciting life*).	☐	☐	☐
... das *present perfect simple* und *present perfect progressive* mit *since* und *for* richtig anwenden. Mit der einfachen Form drücke ich Zustände aus (z.B. *I've known Sam since* 2005). Die Verlaufsform benutze ich bei Handlungen oder Vorgängen (z.B. *I've been walking around for half an hour*). Mit *since* gebe ich einen Zeitpunkt an. Mit *for* gebe ich einen Zeitraum an.	☐	☐	☐
VOKABELVERSTÄNDNIS: Ich kann ...			
... Wörter für Musikinstrumente (z.B. *trumpet, flute, violin*) richtig verwenden.	☐	☐	☐
... 'Transport'-Wörter (z.B. *Tube, ferry, line, bus stop*) richtig verwenden.	☐	☐	☐
... Wörter für Stadt und Land (z.B. *cathedral, coast, bay*) richtig verwenden.	☐	☐	☐
... Wörter für elektronische Medien (z.B. *download, ringtone*) richtig verwenden.	☐	☐	☐
SKILLS – LERNEN UND ARBEITEN: Ich kann ...			
... in einem englisch-deutschen oder deutsch-englischen Wörterbuch ein Wort nachschlagen und die passende Bedeutung finden.	☐	☐	☐
... sinngemäß englische Informationen auf Deutsch und deutsche Informationen auf Englisch wiedergeben, z.B. beim Kauf einer Fahrkarte. Im Englischen nennt man dies *mediation*.	☐	☐	☐

WAS ICH FÜR MEIN ENGLISCHLERNEN GETAN HABE: Ich habe ...	häufig	manchmal	nie
... im Englischunterricht gut aufgepasst und aktiv mitgearbeitet.	☐	☐	☐
... ausprobiert, mit welchen Lern- und Arbeitstechniken ich am besten lernen und arbeiten kann.	☐	☐	☐
... die Aufgaben im Grammar File und Skills File in meinem Buch bearbeitet.	☐	☐	☐

WIE ICH MICH VERBESSERN KÖNNTE: Ich könnte ...

- ... Vokabel- und Grammatikkenntnisse regelmäßig auffrischen. ☐
- ... ein deutsch-englisches Wörterbuch häufiger verwenden. ☐
- ... ausgewählte Workbook-Übungen der Bände 1 und 2 noch einmal bearbeiten. ☐
- ... Texte von meiner CD laut mitlesen, um meine Aussprache und Betonung zu verbessern. ☐
- ... DVDs zuerst auf Deutsch, dann auf Englisch anschauen. ☐
- ... Liedertexte aus dem Internet aufschreiben und mitsingen. ☐

Unit 3 Time for sport

1 My room ▸ p. 54–55

a) *Look carefully at pp. 54–55 of your student's book again. Then read the two descriptions of the room. Which one is correct, A or B? Complete the sentence under the texts ▸.*

A I love my room. It isn't always tidy, but it's comfortable and it's fun. I like bright colours like yellow and blue. But my favourite colour is red – Manchester United's colour. I've got some cool posters on my walls – a Music Festival poster, the United team, of course, and one of a fantastic Caribbean beach. I can dream about it on cold winter days.
My bed is in a corner and my desk is next to it. My desk is usually full of school stuff, papers and books, and my bed and chair are usually full of clothes. My football and my steel drum are near my bed – they're my two favourite things. Do you like my room?

B I have my own room. It's small but I like it. Most of my school stuff, sports gear and my steel drum are in my room. I've got some cool posters on the walls, and the timetable of training sessions for our team. We're in the semi-final! You can easily see that I play football because I've usually got my football and my football shoes right next to my bed – together with my steel drum. There's lots of United stuff too. The poster is great, isn't it? I've got a big wardrobe in my room, but my bed is often full of clothes. I'm a bit untidy. My bed and desk are old, but the blue lamp on my desk is new. Do you like my room?

The correct description of the room is ________ .

▸ I know this because ____

____ .

b) *Draw a picture of your room. Add the window and the furniture.*

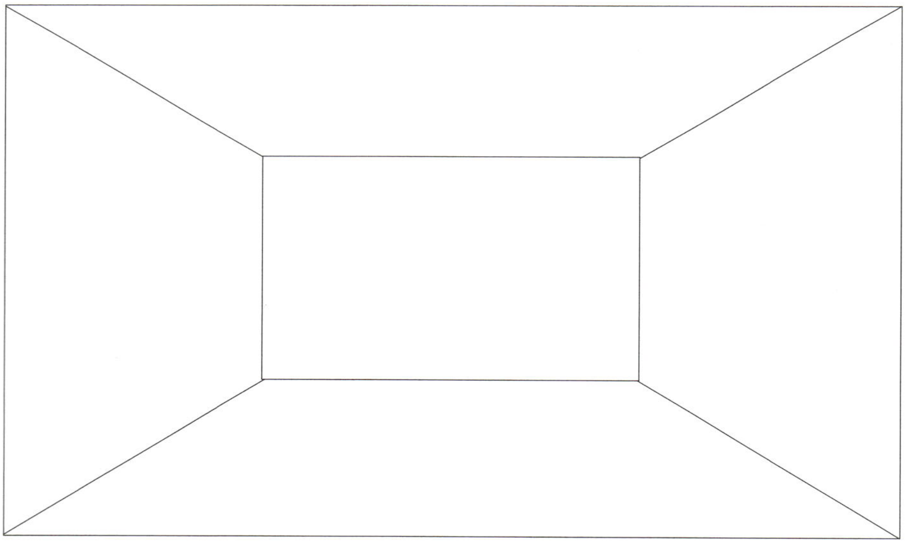

Just for fun

Boy: Dad, I don't need a bike for Christmas any more.
Dad: Why not?
Boy: I found one behind the wardrobe in your room.

c) *Now describe what you see when you open the door of your room. Say where your furniture is: bed, chair, wardrobe, shelves, desk, etc. Use* **on the left/right**, **in a corner**, **near the window**, **behind the door**, *etc. Describe where your things are: books, CDs, clothes, computer, posters, etc. Use* **on the wall**, **near the bed**, **under/behind/next to/between**, *etc. Which things show what you like to do – your hobbies or sports?*

Write three paragraphs in your exercise book.

When you open the door of my room, you see …

2 Blue box: Words without a plural ► p. 55, p. 180

Choose and underline the correct words in the brackets.

1 Do you like my new furniture? – Yes, I think (it's/they're) really cool.
2 Latisha wrote to Katrina: Your news about the film for Scottish TV (are/is) great. Congratulations!
3 Katrina has nice hair. She usually wears (them/it) in a ponytail.
4 Who gave you all (this/these) information about Manchester United? – Latisha, of course!
5 How much homework have we got today? – Not (much/many).

3 WORDS All about ... sport ► p. 56, p. 62/P2, pp. 182–183

Write the missing words. What's the word down ▶?

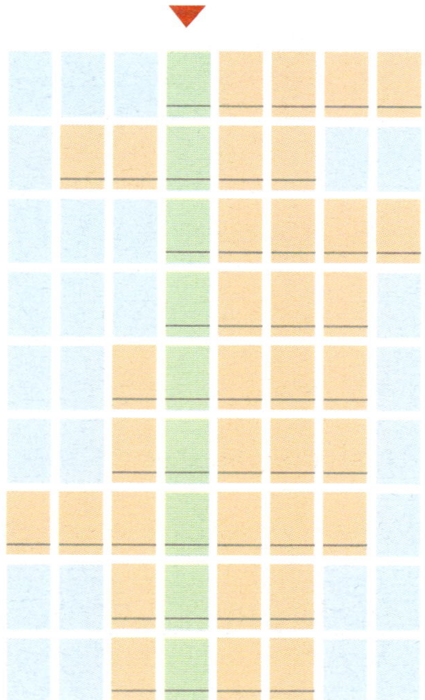

1 What's the ... ? – It's 2–0 (two nil) at the moment.
2 You play tennis and badminton on a ...
3 You play football and hockey on a ...
4 On the half-pipe you need a helmet and ...
5 When Latisha scored, her ... said: 'Not bad.'
6 The U14s usually ... once a week.
7 For jazz dance you wear tights and a ...
8 Latisha says training with her ... is great fun.
9 Manchester United's last match was a ..., 2–2 (two all).

3703 ▶ The word down is another word for 'fan': ______________ .

4 Word field: Sports ► p. 56, p. 62/P2, pp. 182–183

Fill in the missing letters. Then match the words and the pictures.

s a d d le swim _ _ _ _ t _ _ _ ks helm _ _ _ _ _ _ et swim _ _ _ _

c _ _ _ t ru _ _ ing t _ _ _ k ski sl _ _ _ half- _ _ _ _ s _ _ _ _ _ _ ha _ _

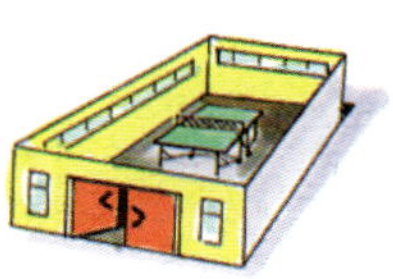

3704

Now you

Do you like sport? What's your favourite sport? Why do you like it best? Are you in a sports team or club? Do you watch sport on TV? Which sports don't you like? Why not?
Write two or three paragraphs in your exercise book.

5 STUDY SKILLS Paraphrasing ▸ p. 57 • SF (p.144)

a) *How does Latisha explain words to Anna? Use* **the same as** *… or* **the opposite of**[1] *… Choose from:*

wet	fan	large	mild	must	terrible

1 What does 'supporter' mean? – Well, it's the same as 'fan'.

2 I don't understand 'dry'. – It's the opposite ____________.

3 What does 'spicy' mean? – It's ____________.

4 And what's 'awful'? – ____________

5 And 'huge'? – ____________

6 And what does 'needn't' mean? – ____________

b) *What's wrong? Write correct sentences to explain the words. Read all the sentences before you start.*

1 A **hairdresser** is somebody who stays at your home to learn your language.
2 A **bridal path** is a place where you play football or hockey.
3 A **saddle** is something that you wear on your head for dangerous sports.
4 An **exchange student** is somebody who cuts hair.
5 A **pitch** is a place where you can ride a horse.
6 A **helmet** is something that you put on a horse before you ride.

1 A hairdresser is ____________.

2 A bridal path is ____________.

3 A saddle is ____________.

4 An exchange student is ____________.

5 A pitch is ____________.

6 A helmet is ____________.

c) *Now explain these German words in English:*

Torwart: ____________

Tischtennis-Schläger: ____________

3805 Tennisplatz: ____________

[1] opposite of ['ɒpəzɪt əf] *Gegenteil von*

6 REVISION Latisha's guest (Full relative clauses)

▸ p. 57 • GF 7a (pp. 154–155)

Complete the text with **who** *for people or* **that** *for things.*

Anna is an exchange student ___who___ is visiting the Byrds. At the moment she's enjoying the meal ___that___ Latisha's mum has made. She has cooked stewed chicken, a dish __________ her grandmother brought from Trinidad. Anna wants to know more about the people __________ came from the Caribbean. Mrs Byrd tells her stories about her grandparents __________ left their home to come to England many years ago. She tells Anna that life wasn't easy for them in a strange country __________ was cold and so different from the Caribbean. She tells her about the problems __________ her grandparents had. Then Latisha says she hasn't got much time for Anna today, but she'll show her everything __________ is interesting tomorrow.

3906

Just for fun

Teacher	Tim, which family does the lion belong to?
Tim	Sorry, Miss. I don't know a family who's got a lion.

7 After dinner (Contact clauses)

▸ p. 57 • GF 7b (pp.155–156)

a) *Find five sentences where you can leave out who or that. Write them again as contact clauses. You need the letters in brackets in part b).*

Anna	The food that your mum cooked was very good, Latisha (m)?
Latisha	Well, now you know plantains are a kind of banana that you have to cook (u). I'm sorry I haven't got much time for you today, Anna.
Anna	That's OK. I know there are other things that are important to you too (l). You want to chat to your friend who lives in Scotland (e). And I know there's some homework that you still have to do (s). And there's your big match on Saturday. I'm afraid football is something that I don't know much about (i). David Beckham is the only English footballer who I know (c).
Latisha	But now you know me too! When you leave Manchester, you'll love football. You'll see!

1 *The food your mum cooked was very good, Latisha.* ___m___

2 ______________________________ ___

3 ______________________________ ___

4 ______________________________ ___

5 ______________________________ ___

3907
3908

b) *Now write down the letters in brackets after your five answers. The letters make a new word.*

▸ If they are correct, the new word tells you one of Anna's favourite hobbies: __________________ .

8 Latisha's things (Full relative clauses or contact clauses)

▸ p. 57 • GF 7 (pp. 154–156)

*Before the big match Latisha is nervous. Make one sentence out of two and write her questions. Use a relative clause with **that/which** or a contact clause where possible.*

1 To her mum: Where's the new team shirt? I got it last Saturday.

Mum, where's the new team shirt I got last Saturday?

2 To Anna: Have you got the ticket? I gave it to you yesterday.

____

3 To her mum: Where are the new white shorts? They were in my wardrobe.

____

4 To her mum: Where are the bananas and the chocolate? I need them for the break.

____

5 To Anna: Have you got that football magazine? It was on my desk.

____

6 To her mum: Remember to take the camera! You're going to film me with it.

____

9 REVISION A training session (Simple past/Present perfect)

▸ p. 57 • GF 1 (p. 149)

Meet Nick. Nick and his friends play in their school football team. Circle the correct verb form in the brackets.

How do you think we'll play in the match next week?
All our supporters will be there. We have to win.

Tony Well, Max (didn't train / hasn't trained) enough.
He (hasn't trained / didn't train) last week. He
(has missed / missed) three training sessions.

Nick When (has he broken / did he break) his leg?

Tony That (was / has been) about six months ago,
in the match against St. Wilfred's.

Luke Well, I agree that he isn't so good at the moment. And what about Andy?
He (hasn't scored / didn't score) any goals in the last match.
And Pete (didn' t play / hasn't played) very well in the match against Parkway last month.
We (lost / have lost) 2 goals to 4, remember?

Nick Well, I (trained / have trained) really hard. I (have been / was) at all our training sessions.
So I hope I'll score a few goals.

Tony That's exactly what Max (said / has said) just before the match when
he (has broken / broke) his leg!

10 WORDS Good or bad? ▸ p. 57

Find adjectives that describe people and feelings. There are 13 words down and 14 across. Make two lists.

y	u	m	m	y	f	s	l	u	c	k	y	e	x	c	i	t	i	n	g
s	p	g	n	f	u	n	n	y	p	b	r	i	p	l	i	a	n	t	d
c	s	i	n	t	e	r	e	s	t	i	n	g	w	o	g	r	e	a	t
a	e	l	e	w	d	e	l	i	c	i	o	u	s	b	b	f	i	n	e
r	t	l	r	o	a	k	h	a	p	p	y	m	h	e	o	h	s	s	u
y	a	a	v	r	f	b	e	a	u	t	i	f	u	l	r	u	t	c	n
m	w	n	o	r	r	d	y	t	x	g	t	i	d	y	i	r	a	a	f
s	f	g	u	i	a	f	a	n	t	a	s	t	i	c	n	t	p	r	a
a	u	r	s	e	i	h	e	a	l	t	h	y	k	s	g	n	i	e	i
d	l	y	l	d	d	q	w	o	n	d	e	r	f	u	l	g	d	d	r

☺ ▸ *yummy,* ______________________

____

☹ ▾ *scary,* ______________________

____

11 What's done? (Passive: simple present) ▸ p. 58 • GF 8a–c (pp. 156–157)

What happens before a big football match? What happens during the match? Complete the text with verbs in the simple present passive.

A lot of work *is done* (do) before a football match. A big match __________ (prepare) months before it __________ (play). When the date __________ (announce), tickets __________ (sell) at ticket places or on the internet. On the day of the match, often earlier, souvenirs __________ (buy), everything from T-shirts to teddy bears in the colours of the teams. The pitch __________ (prepare) for the big day. Sometimes a player __________ (hurt) badly and __________ (take) to hospital. But goals __________ (score) and after 90 minutes the match __________ (lose) or __________ (win). If it's a big final, a cup __________ (present).

Info box

People played a sport like football 3000 years ago in Japan, and later in Greece and Rome. In England, three kings and Queen Elizabeth I banned[1] football because it was very noisy. There were as many as 21 players on each side and players usually left the game with broken legs! From 1870 the rules[2] allowed only 11 players for each team. Now football is the game that is played and watched most all over the world.

[1] ban [bæn] *verbieten* [2] rule [ru:l] *Regel*

4111

12 Uranus was discovered by ... (Passive with by: simple past)

► p. 59 • GF 8d (p. 157)

Is the information right or wrong? If you are unsure, use the internet for help. Use passive sentences with **by** *in your answers.*

1 Brunel designed and built the Clifton Suspension Bridge in Bristol.

Right. The Clifton Suspension Bridge in Bristol was designed and built by Brunel.

2 Alexander Fleming discovered the planet Uranus.

Wrong.

3 Alexander Graham Bell invented[1] the telephone.

4 John Logie Baird discovered penicillin[2] in 1929.

5 Sir Norman Foster designed and built 'The Gherkin' in 2003.

6 Michael Jackson wrote and sang the hit song 'We will rock you'.

7 L.S. Lowry painted the Mona Lisa.

4212

13 REVISION Quick quiz

► p. 59

Read the questions and write the question words in the puzzle. Can you complete it in one minute?

1 _ _ _ ... is going to watch the match?

2 _ _ _ _ ... does it start?

3 _ _ _ _ _ ... programme is it on? BBC1?

4 _ _ _ _ _ ... are they playing? Wembley?

5 _ _ _ _ _ ... favourite team is United? Yours?

6 _ _ _ _ ... will happen if they lose? – They won't!

7 _ _ _ ... many goals do you think they'll score?

8 _ _ _ ... don't we all watch the match together?

4213

[1] invent [in'vent] *erfinden* [2] penicillin [ˌpenɪ'sɪlɪn] *Penizillin*

14 WRITING COURSE Part 3: Collecting and organizing ideas (A report)

▸ p. 59 • SF (p. 147)

a) *What is important when you write a report on a sport event or other event? Tick (✔) the correct boxes.*

- Give quick information ☒
- Give details first ☐
- Give important information first ☒
- Say how the weather was, etc. ☐
- Give information about the '5 Ws' + *How?* ☒
- Always give information in the same order: *Who? What? When? Where? Why? + How?* ☐
- Structure your information in a mind map or a table ☒

b) *A young reporter is writing a short report about Nick's school match for a newspaper. How can you make the report better? What should stay in the report? Mark the sentences blue. What should the reporter leave out? Mark the sentences red.*

Rosehill Park School played against St. Joseph's Catholic School in Bridgeford last Saturday. It was cold for the time of the year. There wasn't much sun and there were some dark clouds. It was the schools' cup final. The match started ten minutes late.

Both teams made a fast start. The first goal was scored in the 29th minute by St. Joseph's captain, Luke Newman. At half-time the score was still 0–1 for St. Joseph's. It rained a bit in the break. In an exciting second half, Rosehill's captain Nick Scott was fouled. He took the penalty and equalized. A second goal for Rosehill Park was scored in the 89th minute, again by Nick Scott. St. Joseph's were tired and made mistakes. Their team captain argued with the goalkeeper.

The final score was 2–1 for Rosehill, who were the stronger team. Nick Scott's mum is going to buy him a new football. The cup was presented by footballer Michael Ashley, a TV celebrity. He had a bad cold. The match was watched by a large crowd of students, parents and teachers.

c) *Now write the final report.*

15 PRONUNCIATION Different stress in English and German words ▸ p. 59 🎧6

a) *Mark the stress on the German words. Then listen and mark the stress on the English words.*

	English		German		English		German
1	accent	–	Akzent	6	moment	–	Moment
2	discussion	–	Diskussion	7	national	–	national
3	electricity	–	Elektrizität	8	parliament	–	Parlament
4	information	–	Information	9	realistic	–	realistisch
5	million	–	Million	10	transport	–	Transport

4415 ***b)*** *Find the word with the same stress in German and English. Draw a ☺ next to it.*

Fun fact

At the Wimbledon Tennis Championship[1] 42,000 tennis balls are used in two weeks!

16 LISTENING An interview ▸ p. 59 🎧7

Meet Nicola and her brother Calvin. They both play great tennis, but not just for fun. They want to become top junior national players. First, listen to the whole interview. Then listen again and underline the correct answers.

1 How old is Nicola? (14 / 15)

2 How old is Calvin? (15 / 16)

3 When did Nicola begin to play tennis? (when she was 8 / 8 years ago)

4 How long have they both been playing tennis? (for six years / for eight years)

5 How often do they train? (every day/ Monday to Saturday)

6 What do they do on Sundays? (they watch TV all day / they do homework)

7 Who do they train with? (with their father / with their coach)

8 Who already has four junior titles? (Nicola / Calvin)

9 Where is Calvin going to play next weekend? (Brighton / Bournemouth / London)

10 How many junior titles has Calvin got at the moment? (3 / 4)

11 What does Nicola want to be if she doesn't become a top junior player? (a doctor / a sports teacher)

12 What does Calvin want to be if he doesn't become a top junior player? (a tennis coach / an engineer)

[1] championship ['tʃæmpiənʃɪp] *Meisterschaft*

17 Words that go together

▸ p. 59

a) *Find a verb from the box that you can use with all the words. Then add one word (or more) to each list. Use the dictionary on pp. 193–220 of your student's book for help.*

do • have • keep • make • *ride* • take

1 You *ride* a bike, a horse, *a camel* .

2 You ________ warm, in touch, ________ .

3 You ________ care, a part, ________ .

4 You ________ a cake, a mess, ________ .

5 You ________ homework, tricks, ________ .

6 You ________ a shower, a sore throat, ________ .

b) *Write a sentence with each verb.*

1 *I have never ridden a camel, but I think it would be fun.*

2 ____________________

3 ____________________

4 ____________________

5 ____________________

4517 6 ____________________

18 Extra Background File MANCHESTER

▸ pp. 60–61

What do you know about Manchester?

a) *Answer the questions from the information on pp. 60–61 of your student's book and from the internet.*

1 What is Manchester most famous for?

Manchester is probably most famous for Manchester United and Old Trafford.

2 How many famous football teams has Manchester got? What are their names?

____

____

3 What is Old Trafford?

____

____

4 There's a second Old Trafford. What do you know about it?

____

5 What made Manchester rich in the 19th century?

____

b) *Choose one of these topics. Collect information from your student's book and from the internet. Then write two or three paragraphs in your exercise book.*

1 Old Trafford   2 Manchester's history   3 Music in Manchester

19 WORKING WITH THE TEXT Who needs legs? ▸ pp. 69–70

a) *Read p. 69 of your student's book (again). Then write questions about Nathan.*

1 Where *was Nathan born?* – In a village in Wales.

2 When ____________ ? – On 11th April 1988.

3 What did ____________ ? – He learned to ride.

4 What ____________ ? – He got some riding boots and a riding hat.

5 Who ____________ ? – Some cousins and friends.

6 Where ____________ ? – They went to the old railway line.

7 What ____________ ? – He tried to jump onto a train.

b) *Now read p. 70 of your student's book. Scan the text and put these events in the correct order (1–7):*

He started to play sledge hockey. ☐

He won three gold medals at the Junior British Championships. ☐

He played hockey for Great Britain. ☐

Nathan played football at school. *1*

He represented Wales at the Commonwealth Games in Melbourne. ☐

He started to do athletics in summer. ☐

He wants to be in the next Paralympics. ☐

c) *Put the words from the story in the puzzle and find the word down.*

1 A kind of doctor.

2 Running, jumping and throwing are part of this.

3 You can sit on this and ride down a slope with snow.

4 If you're in a wheelchair you are ...

5 If you're hurt, you go to hospital in this.

6 Nathan ... his country in the Paralympics.

1		_	_	_	_	_	_	_	_	_
2		_	_	_	_	_	_	_	_	_
3			_	_	_	_	_	_		
4			_	_	_	_	_	_	_	_
5		_	_	_	_	_	_	_	_	_
6	_	_	_	_	_	_	_	_	_	_

▸ Nathan has won lots of these: ____________ .

d) *In your exercise book, write a paragraph about Nathan's hopes for the future. Start like this:*

Nathan is full of hope for the future because ...

1 What are they? Write the names.

1 g____________

2 ____________

3 ____________

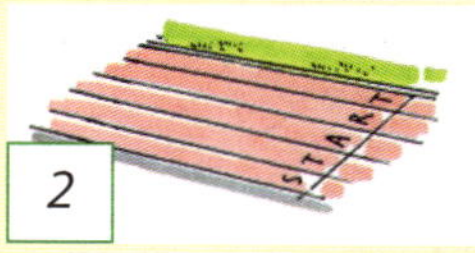

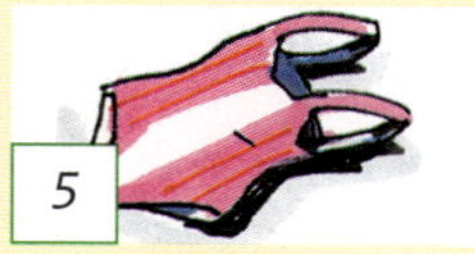

4 ____________

5 ____________

6 ____________

4701

2 Paraphrasing

Explain the words in English. Use ***who***, ***that*** *or a contact clause. Choose from the box.*

stops the ball in the goal • shows paintings and interesting art • girls wear for jazz dance

1 Galerie: It's a place ____________.

2 Gymnastikanzug: It's something ____________.

4702 *3* Torwart: It's the player ____________.

3 Complete with the passive: simple present or simple past

1 The Lowry Centre ____________ (open) in 2000.

2 The Lowry ____________ (name) after a famous painter.

3 Lots of Lowry's paintings ____________ (show) in the galleries.

4703 *4* Manchester's oldest buildings ____________ (build) in the 15th century.

4 Complete the text with 'sports' words.

Rosehill ____________ St. Joseph's in the schools' football cup ____________ in Bridgeford last Saturday.

At ____________ the ____________ was 0–1 for St. Joseph's. After the break Rosehill's captain

Nick Scott was ____________ by St. Joseph's captain. He took the ____________ and scored

4704 his second ____________ in the 89th minute.

20 points

Now you

If you were an exchange student in Manchester, what would you like to see and do? Write two paragraphs in your exercise book. Remember to use topic sentences.

4705
4706 *If I was an exchange student in Manchester, I think I would like to see Old Trafford because ...*

Unit 4 Growing up in Canada

1 What do you know about Canada? ▸ pp. 72–73

a) Are the statements right or wrong? Tick (✓) the correct boxes and write the letters below▸.

	Right	Wrong
1 Germany is as big as Canada.	Q	M
2 For First Nations people, hunting and fishing are very important.	O	U
3 The city of Toronto has more snow than the town of Inuvik.	E	N
4 It is colder in Inuvik than in Toronto or Berlin.	T	B
5 Canada has lots of lakes and mountains.	R	E
6 One of Canada's favourite summer sports is cricket.	K	E
7 The population of Canada is larger than the population of Germany.	L	A
8 Nickelback is a Canadian rock group.	L	A

▸ If your answers are correct, you have written the name of a Canadian city where French is spoken.

The city is ______________________________ .

b) Answer the questions.

1 Which sports and activities do lots of Canadians do?

Canadians like to go ______________________________

______________________________ .

2 Which two main languages are spoken in Canada?

____

3 Which city is not in Canada: Toronto, Montréal, Wellington, Winnipeg?

____

4 Which singer is Canadian: Robbie Williams, Avril Lavigne, Shakira, Beyoncé Knowles?

____

____

5 Canadian kids love sleepovers. What do kids do at a sleepover?

At a sleepover kids ______________________________

____

2 REVISION Canada facts (Passive) ▸ p. 75 • GF 8 (pp. 156–157)

*Write sentences in the passive. Use the simple present, sometimes with **by**.*

1 Canada – visit – about 300,000 German tourists every year

Canada is visited by 300,000 German tourists every year.

2 Two main languages – speak – in Canada: English and French

____

3 Ice hockey – play – lots of Canadians – in winter

____

4 Black bears – find – in forests in all parts of Canada

____

4902

Info box

It is believed that Canada has almost 2 million lakes. 32,000 of them have an area of at least 3 square kilometres!

3 WORDS All about … teenagers and adults ▸ p. 75

a) *Complete the sentences with these words:*

argue | spend | strict | views | waste

1 Teenagers and parents often *argue* .

2 The reason is that they have different ______________ on money.

3 Adults think teenagers ______________ too much money. Adults say that money doesn't grow on trees.

4 Adults think teenagers ______________ a lot of time.

5 Teenagers often think their parents are too ______________ .

b) *Read p. 74 of your student's book again. What do teenagers often like to do? Write a short paragraph. Use all the words from the box in your text:*

cellphones · chat · fashions · hang out · shopping malls · sleepovers · text · trendy

____

____

____

____

____

4903

Now you

Teenagers are not all the same. What about you? Which of the things in b) do you like doing? Which don't you like doing? Write two paragraphs in your exercise book. Remember to structure your text.

4 REVISION More Canada facts (Relative clauses) ▸ p. 75 • GF 7 (pp. 154–156)

*Complete the sentences with **who** or **that**. Use a contact clause where possible.*

1 Canada is a country (that) ______ lots of German tourists visit every year.

2 Inuvik is a town in the north of Canada ______ has snow from September to May.

3 There are lots of famous Canadians. Shania Twain is a famous singer ______ was born in Canada.

4 French is the language ______ is spoken by almost 7 million Canadians.

5 People ______ live in Canada and speak French are called French-Canadians.

5004 6 Dragon boat racing is a sport ______ many Canadians do in summer.

5 After school had finished (Past perfect) ▸ p. 75 • GF 9 (p. 158)

*What did Robert do last Wednesday after school had finished? Make one sentence out of two. Begin with **After** ... and use the past perfect.*

First ...	Then ...
1 School finished.	Robert went to the local mall.
2 He walked up and down the mall.	He went into a CD shop.
3 Robert looked at CDs for a few minutes.	Sam arrived.
4 Robert bought a present for Ashley.	He and Sam left the shop.
5 They looked at new computer games.	They went for an ice cream.

1 After school had finished, Robert went to the local mall.

2 After he ______

3 ______

4 ______

5005 5 ______

Now you

*Write four sentences about last Saturday. Begin with **After** ... and use the past perfect.*

After I had got up, I had my breakfast. After I had got ready to go out, I ______

______

______

______

______

______

______

6 An e-mail from Robert (Simple past and past perfect) ▸ p. 75 • GF 9–10a (pp. 158–159)

Complete Robert's e-mail to Asif with verbs in the simple past or past perfect.

Hi Asif!

I hope your day was better than mine!

In the first lesson I realized (realize) that I had forgotten (forgot) to do my English homework. The teacher ______ (ask) me why I ______ (not do) it. I couldn't tell her that I ______ (DJ) at the youth centre until 11 o'clock the night before. She ______ (give) me extra homework! What a bummer! After school I ______ (buy) the new Avril Lavigne CD, but at home I ______ (realize) that I ______ (leave) the bag on the bus. Dad ______ (be) angry because I ______ (leave) my cellphone at school. My mom was angry because I ______ (not tidy) my room. I ______ (plan) to meet friends and go to the cinema, but after I ______ (do) the extra homework it ______ (be) too late. Now I'm happy that it's time to go to bed!

5106

7 REVISION What was happening at the party? (Past progressive) ▸ p. 75 • GF 10a (p. 159)

What was happening when Robert arrived? Look at the picture, then write sentences in the past progressive.

1 When Robert arrived, Ashley was looking at her presents.

2 ... Sam ______.

3 ... Ben and Lisa ______.

4 ... Trish ______.

5 ... Nick und Sandy ______.

5107 6 ... Marie ______.

8 Party chat (Indirect speech) ► p. 77 • GF 11 (pp. 160–161)

Report what people at the party said.

1
Nickelback songs are fantastic to dance to.

2
It's a pity that Emily hasn't come.

3
I've often heard DJ Bobby at the youth centre.

4
My parents have given me money for a trip to Ottawa.

5
I'll ask Robert to DJ at my next party.

1 Jessica *said Nickelback songs were fantastic to dance to.*

2 Robert ______________________________.

3 Jordan ______________________________.

4 Ashley ______________________________.

5 Jessica ______________________________.

Fun fact

Vancouver is one of the few cities in the world where you can play golf, swim in the sea and go skiing all in one day!

9 Tourists in Canada (Indirect speech) ► p. 77 • GF 11 (pp. 160–161)

Report what tourists at Toronto Airport said/told the interviewer about Canada and their holiday there.

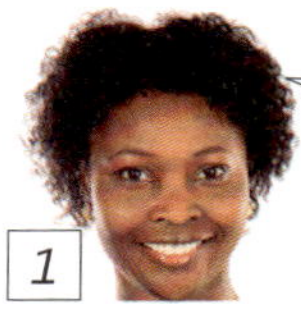
1
The Canadian people are so friendly, and Canada is such a clean country.

2
I love Vancouver. I think it's the most beautiful city in the world.

3
We've been to see Niagara Falls again. They're amazing.

4
We've visited three national parks and seen ten black bears.

5
The scenery is fantastic. I know I'll come again in my next holidays.

1 A woman said *the Canadian people were so friendly, and Canada was such a clean country.*

2 A man told the interviewer that ______________________________

3 A couple said ______________________________

4 A boy told the interviewer that ______________________________

5 Another man said ______________________________

5209

10 About Algonquin Park (Indirect speech) ▸ *p. 77 • GF 11 (pp. 160–161)*

A man at the Algonquin visitor centre gave Ted, a British tourist, this information. Ted reported the gist to his family. Match the direct and the reported statements.

The man at the visitor centre said ...

- If you like scenery. Algonquin is the place to be. 7630 square kilometres of forests, rivers and lakes.
- We get about a million visitors every year. In 2007 we had the most ever.
- You'll have a great time. The kids will love the wildlife[1]. Get up early and maybe you'll see black bears, deer, squirrels, raccoons – 53 different kinds of animals and 272 kinds of birds.
- You can do a canoe[2] trip – we've got 2000 km of canoe routes – and 2400 lakes.
- We haven't heard of any bear attacks[3] for years. Just do what the signs say and be careful with food.

Ted reported ...

- He told me it was pretty safe. They hadn't heard of any bear attacks for a long time. He said we should just read the signs and be careful.
- He thought the kids would love the wildlife, but he said we had to get up early to see bears.
- He said we could go canoeing and swimming everywhere – there were over 2000 lakes.
- He said Algonquin was the place to be if we liked lakes and forests.
- He told me over a million tourists came to Algonquin every year. In 2007 they had had the most visitors ever.

11 WORDS Puzzle ▸ *p. 77*

Complete the puzzle and find the word down ▸.

1 Another word for 'answer' is ...
2 *Sam:* Ashley doesn't care about anything. She's one ... girl.
3 The speed limit is 50 miles ... hour.
4 Sometimes ... don't seem to understand what kids like to do.
5 After school Robert met Sam in the shopping ...
6 Sam had to go to ... boat training.
7 Sam had to paddle the boat, not ... it. That was his uncle's job.
8 ... Robert, Sam had never paddled a boat before.
9 Robert DJs at his ... youth centre.
10 Are people still allowed to ... bears in Canada?

5311

▸ Canada's ______________________ is about 34 million.

[1] wildlife ['waɪldlaɪf] *Tier- und Pflanzenwelt* [2] canoe [kə'nu] *Kanu* [3] attack [ə'tæk] *Angriff*

12 WRITING COURSE Part 4: The steps of writing

▸ p. 77, p. 85/P 13 • SF (pp. 146–147)

a) *Look at p. 85 of your student's book again and complete the sentences.*

The three steps of writing are *prewriting* ______________ and ______________.

1 In Step 1 you ______________ That means: ______________

______________ Then you choose ______________

and ______________.

You can do this with a ______________ or a ______________ Use the 5 ______________ and ______________.

2 In Step 2 you ______________ in ______________ parts. The story should have a ______________

____

3 Step 3 is ______________. That means: ______________

____

b) *Now match. Which statements go with which step? Write 1, 2 or 3 after the sentences.*

1 Prewriting	2 Writing	3 Revising

- Brainstorm your ideas [*1*]
- Check the spelling [ ]
- Use adjectives (*hungry*, *beautiful*) and adverbs (*really*, *very*, *quickly*, *well*) [ ]
- Answer the 5 Ws (*Who*, *What*, *When*, *Where*, *Why* and *How*) [ ]
- Check for mistakes (verb forms, word order) [ ]
- Find a title [ ]
- Make a mind map or a chart of ideas [ ]
- Use time phrases (*in the afternoon*, *before breakfast*) [ ]
- Check the order of events. Is it clear? [ ]
- Use linking words (*but*, *so*, *because*) [ ]
- Give your story a beginning, a middle and an end [ ]

c) *Here's the beginning of a story about a camping trip.*

It was a hot week at the beginning of August. Jordan and his dad wanted to do a camping trip together, because they both enjoyed climbing and looking for animals. So they went to Algonquin Park for a few days. Jordan's cousin Dave went with them.

How can the story continue? In your exercise book, write the middle of the story in the simple past. Use the information in b) and these notes, or use your own ideas.

The first night – all tired – sleep well / Next morning Dave – get up early – walk – wash room on campground[1] / Jordan and dad – wait a long time, but Dave – not come / Jordan and dad – worried – look for Dave – not there / Jordan and dad – go – wash room / On the way there – find – Dave's towel and soap – path / Suddenly – feel scared / accident – bear?

d) *Think of an exciting or interesting ending. Maybe you can think of a good explanation why Dave had disappeared. Write the ending in your exercise book and give the story a title.*

[1] campground ['kæmp,graʊnd] *Zeltplatz*

13 LISTENING The CN Tower ▸ p. 77 8

Robert's cousin Emma from Vancouver is staying in Toronto. The Smiths are going to take her up the CN Tower. Robert and his dad are telling her about it. Before you start, read the 14 statements. Then listen carefully and tick (✓) the correct box.

	Right	Wrong	Don't know
1 CN means 'Canadian National'.	☐	☐	☐
2 The Tower is visited by more than 2 million tourists every year.	☐	☐	☐
3 The Tower is 535 metres high.	☐	☐	☐
4 There are ten high-speed elevators which take you to the top in 58 seconds.	☐	☐	☐
5 The elevators don't go if it's raining.	☐	☐	☐
6 The Tower was built ten years ago.	☐	☐	☐
7 There are 1,176 stairs to the top.	☐	☐	☐
8 People can climb the stairs twice a year to collect money for charity.	☐	☐	☐
9 The fastest climb was in 1989 – in 7 minutes 52 seconds.	☐	☐	☐
10 Two men once carried[1] up a dishwasher, a fridge and a cooker.	☐	☐	☐
11 In 1981 a man climbed up the stairs 17 times in one day.	☐	☐	☐
12 There's the famous Glass Floor, 342 metres up.	☐	☐	☐
13 The Glass Floor can hold 25 large hippos!	☐	☐	☐
14 Emma doesn't want to look through the Glass Floor.	☐	☐	☐

Now you

In your exercise book, write some facts about the Tower and say what visitors can see and do there.

14 STUDY SKILLS Mediation ▸ p. 77 • SF (pp. 143–144)

a) *You are in a national park with your family. You see a park ranger[2] and your parents would like to ask him some questions. What do you say? Your dad says to you:*

Frag ihn,
- ob wir hier in der Nähe unser Zelt aufschlagen dürfen.
- was wir mit unserem Abfall machen sollen.
- ob man Angelruten ausleihen kann.

Info box

Black bears can live 21 to 33 years. They can run as fast as horses and can smell maybe 100 times better than people.

b) *Paraphrase: 1 Zelt 2 Abfall 3 Angelrute*

1 ______________________________

2 ______________________________

5514 *3* ______________________________

[1] carry ['kæri] *tragen* [2] ranger ['reɪndʒə] *Aufseher/in*

15 REVISION Chat with Robert and Asif (Simple past/Present perfect) ▸ p. 77 • GF 1 (p. 149)

Write the correct verb form. Simple past or present perfect?

Asif Hi Robert! I need your help! I have just done (just, do) a school project about Canada's animals. Now I need some cool photos of bears. I hope that you __________ (take) some that you could send me. __________ (you, ever, see) a grizzly[1]?

Robert Only in the zoo. I __________ (not meet) a wild one yet – lucky for me. They live high up in the mountains. But my dad __________ (see) a grizzly. Last year on a walking trip in the mountains with a friend he suddenly __________ (see) this huge grizzly, right in front of them, not 30 metres away!

Asif Wow! And __________ (your dad, take) a photo?

Robert You're joking! Dad __________ (feel) so scared that he couldn't move at first. Luckily, the bear __________ (not seem) to be very interested in him.

Asif Or maybe the bear just __________ (not be) very hungry!

16 REVISION How long ...? (Present perfect progressive with since/for) ▸ p. 77 • GF 3, 10b (pp. 151–159)

*Ask questions with **How long** ... and complete the answers with **since** or **for**.*

1 Jordan does judo.

How long has he been doing judo?

For about two years.

2 Ashley does jazzdance.

How long __________?

__________ January last year.

3 Robert DJs at parties.

____

__________ over a year.

4 Jordan plays in a band.

____

__________ he got a new guitar.

5 Sam is learning to paddle a dragon boat.

____

Only __________ a few days.

5616

[1] grizzly (bear) ['grɪzli (beə)] *Grislibär*

17 Extra Background File CANADA ▸ pp. 78–79

a) *What have you learned about Canada? Circle the correct answer, A, B or C. If you are not sure, look at pp. 78–79 of your student's book again. You need the letters in brackets in part b).*

1 The first Europeans in Canada were …

A the Romans. (H)	B the Vikings. (O)	C the French. (S)

2 Canada's biggest city is …

A Ottawa. (O)	B Toronto. (A)	C Montréal. (B)

3 Canada has an aboriginal population of about …

A 4.4 %. (R)	B 4.5 %. (K)	C 5.4 %. (E)

4 Who took Canada from the French in 1763?

A The Germans. (K)	B The British. (E)	C The Americans. (S)

5 'Nunavut' means …

A happy land. (E)	B new land. (T)	C our land. (S)

6 Where is Toronto?

A In Québec. (Y)	B In British Columbia. (E)	C In Ontario. (C)

7 Nunavut is as big as …

A western Europe. (S)	B eastern Europe. (G)	C Ontario. (H)

8 Canada's first Nobel Prize was won by …

A Margaret Atwood. (A)	B Frederick Banting. (L)	C John Cabot. (Y)

b) *Now write the letters in brackets next to your answers in the boxes below. If your answers are correct, the letters make the name of a Canadian sport. Here are the question numbers:*

8	2	6	3	1	5	7	4
				O			

c) *Tell a friend two interesting facts about each of these topics:*
1 First Nations people 2 The history of Canada 3 Immigration to Canada 4 National sports

1 ______________________________

____

2 ______________________________

____

3 ______________________________

____

4 ______________________________

____

18 WORKING WITH THE TEXT A fishing trip ▸ pp. 87–88

a) *Which caption goes with which picture? Match and write a caption under each picture.*

A dangerous accident | The evening before the trip | A good start to the fishing trip

Oh no! Is this the end? | Which is the best way to go? | ~~Will the bear run to the fish?~~

A

Will the bear run to the fish?

B

____

C

____

D

____

E

____

F

____

b) *What do you think people in the pictures are saying? Match the speech bubbles to the pictures.*

"Looks like a nice one there, son!"

Picture ____

"Wow, the river is high. I've never seen rapids like this. I say we go through on the right."

Picture ____

"Are you OK? Dad! You've got a cut on your head. Grab the canoe, Dad."

Picture ____

"Why are you just standing there, bear? Go and get that fish!"

Picture ____

"Calm down, Robert. OK, stay close to me. We have to stay together. We look bigger like this."

Picture ____

"Even if we had electricity, Robert, there's no TV or internet out here in the woods."

Picture ____

1 Complete the words.

1 Toronto has a p__________ of about 2.5 million.

2 The Indians of Canada are called the F__________ .

3 Are people allowed to h__________ bears in Canada?

4 Some bears w__________ 150 kilograms or more.

5901 *5* Sam couldn't p__________ a canoe, but his uncle taught him.

2 Underline the correct verb form.

1 After Robert and his dad (were/had been) in their canoes for about half an hour, they (had stopped/stopped) to try to catch fish.

2 Robert felt excited because he (caught/had caught) a big fish.

3 After the accident Mr Smith couldn't paddle because he (broke/had broken) his foot.

5902 *4* They (just reached/had just reached) the old bridge when they (had seen/saw) the bear again.

3 Fill in the missing word.

1 What kind of things do __________ and teenagers argue about?

2 Teenagers often think their parents are too __________ .

3 Jordan does judo, band practice and __________ work in his free time.

4 Robert DJs at the __________ youth centre.

5903 *5* Teenagers like to meet friends after school, often in shopping __________ .

4 What did Robert tell Sam after the party?

1 Everyone really enjoyed the party.

2 Jessica wants me to DJ at her party.

3 We're driving up to the cabin soon.

4 I'll call again when we get home.

1 Robert said __________ .

2 He told Sam __________ .

3 He said __________ .

5904 *4* He told Sam __________ .

20 points

Now you

5905 *If you went on holiday to Canada, what would you like to see and do there?*

5906 *Write a few paragraphs in your exercise book. Ideas: Cities, sights, animals, sports*

Here are some exercises that will help you with your practice test 2.

1 STUDY SKILLS Understanding new words

► *pp. 90–91 • SF (p. 134)*

Guess what these new words mean in German. Then check your answers in an English-German dictionary.

1 careless ____________________

2 footprint ____________________

3 imagination ____________________

4 improvement ____________________

5 safety ____________________

6 survivor ____________________

2 Spelling (German and English words)

► *pp. 90–91*

Write the English word.

1 Titel – title

2 Kalender – ____________________

3 Tipp – ____________________

4 Theater – ____________________

5 Temperatur – ____________________

6 Adresse – ____________________

7 Diskussion – ____________________

8 Telefon – ____________________

9 Programm – ____________________

10 Kathedrale – ____________________

3 WRITING Organizing ideas (The 5 Ws and How?)

► *pp. 90–91 • SF (p. 147)*

a) *Read a part of Robert's e-mail to Asif. First, mark the sentence parts that give answers to the '5 Ws' and How?*

I must tell you about our last big trip. We went to Vancouver on the west coast. It's a long way from Toronto so we can't go there often. I've only been there twice. The last time was in August, in the school holidays. It's too far to drive there, so we – my parents, me and my grandma from Toronto – went by plane. Grandma was more excited than I was!
We went to visit family – and to enjoy the city, of course. My Uncle Joe, Aunt Stacey and two cousins live near Vancouver. We saw all the city sights – Stanley Park and the Aquarium ...,

b) *Now write down the information in the e-mail that answers the questions:*

What? our last big trip

When? ____________________

Where? ____________________

Who? ____________________

Why? ____________________

How? ____________________

4 Robert and his friends (Word order) ▸ pp. 90–91

Write correct sentences.

1 often/DJs/at the community hall/Robert/on Friday evenings

Robert often DJs at the community hall on Friday evenings.

2 went/Jessica/to get/to the shopping mall/for Ashley/a present

____

3 When/computer games/for hours/Emily/plays/gets angry/her mom

____

4 the bear hunt/Sam/thinks/needs/that/Ontario

____

5 often/to their cabin/Robert and his parents/drive/for the weekend

____

6 were/scared/Robert and his dad/really/because/followed/a bear/them

____

5 Latisha and Anna (Simple past and present perfect) ▸ pp. 90–91 • GF 1 (p. 149)

a) *Underline the correct verb form.*

1 Latisha (has played/played) for Manchester United U14s for two years. They (won/have won) their last match.

2 Anna (wasn't/hasn't been) on a student exchange before. This is her first time.

3 Anna knows that Latisha plays football, but she (hasn't seen/didn't see) her on the pitch yet.

4 On Anna's first evening with the Byrds, Latisha's mum (made/has made) stewed chicken.

b) *Now report what Latisha and Anna did on Saturday. Use the simple past.*

1 Latisha didn't have (not have) time for Anna on the first evening, but on Saturday morning she __________ (take) her to the Lowry.

2 Latisha __________ (explain) to Anna, 'L. S. Lowry __________ (be) an artist.

He __________ (paint) pictures. He __________ (not work) in a circus.'

3 In the afternoon, Anna __________ (not want) to watch football, but she __________ (go) to Latisha's match.

4 When Latisha __________ (score) the final goal, Anna __________ (be) very excited.

5 On the next day Latisha __________ (see) her name in the newspaper and her mum __________ (feel) very proud.

Jetzt kann ich ...	Sehr gut!	OK	Verbessern!
HÖREN: Ich kann ...			
... längere Texte und Geschichten verstehen, auch wenn mir einige Wörter nicht bekannt sind.	☐	☐	☐
... aus Listening-Übungen Details (z.B. Zahlen) richtig heraushören.	☐	☐	☐
... den Akzent britischer und kanadischer Sprecher/innen heraushören.	☐	☐	☐
... die Wörter der Units 3 und 4 verstehen.	☐	☐	☐
SPRECHEN: Ich kann ...			
... mein Zimmer (z.B. Möbel, Einrichtungsgegenstände) beschreiben.	☐	☐	☐
... meine Meinung zu Themen wie z.B. Musik, Probleme zwischen Teenagern und Eltern frei äußern, auch wenn ich Fehler mache.	☐	☐	☐
... über Sportarten, Sportereignisse und den Spielstand berichten.	☐	☐	☐
... *songs* beschreiben und meine Meinung dazu äußern.	☐	☐	☐
... Wörter, die im Englischen und im Deutschen ähnlich sind, richtig betonen (z.B. *'programme, 'concert*).	☐	☐	☐
... die Wörter der Units 3 und 4 richtig aussprechen und anwenden.	☐	☐	☐
LESEN: Ich kann ...			
... einen Bericht über ein Sportereignis (z.B. über ein Fußballspiel) lesen und verstehen.	☐	☐	☐
... die längeren Texte und Dialoge der Units 3 und 4 lesen und verstehen.	☐	☐	☐
... die längeren Texte und Dialoge der Units 3 und 4 ohne Probleme laut lesen.	☐	☐	☐
SCHREIBEN: Ich kann ...			
... ein *profile* über einen Freund/eine Freundin schreiben.	☐	☐	☐
... einen kurzen Bericht über ein Sportereignis schreiben. Dabei beginne ich mit wichtigen Informationen und decke die 5 Ws ab.	☐	☐	☐
... mithilfe von sprachlichen Mitteln eine Geschichte zu Ende schreiben.	☐	☐	☐
... Fragen zu Texten der Units 3 und 4 schriftlich beantworten.	☐	☐	☐
... die Wörter der Units 3 und 4 richtig schreiben.	☐	☐	☐
LAND UND LEUTE: Ich ...			
... weiß, dass Manchester (UK) eine wichtige Stadt für Sport und die Heimatstadt der Fußballmannschaft *Manchester United* ist.	☐	☐	☐
... kenne die Namen einiger Sehenswürdigkeiten in Manchester (z.B. *Old Trafford, the Lowry, Salford Quays*).	☐	☐	☐
... habe einiges über Kanada sowie über die Stadt Toronto gelernt (z.B. Bevölkerung, Größe, Landschaft, Klima).	☐	☐	☐
... habe einiges über den kanadischen Lebensstil gelernt (z.B. beliebte Sportarten, das Freizeitverhalten kanadischer Teenager).	☐	☐	☐

Jetzt kann ich …	**Sehr gut!**	**OK**	**Verbessern!**
GRAMMATIKVERSTÄNDNIS: Ich kann …			
… einige Nomen, die im Englischen keine Pluralform haben, richtig verwenden (z.B. *furniture/homework/information/news is…*).	☐	☐	☐
… *relative pronouns* für Personen (*who*) und Sachen (*that/which*) sowie *contact clauses* richtig verwenden (z.B. *That's the boy I met at the party*).	☐	☐	☐
… den Unterschied zwischen einem Aktiv- und einem Passivsatz erkennen und das Passiv im *simple present* und im *simple past* richtig bilden (z.B. *The Lowry is named after a famous painter/It was opened in 2000*).	☐	☐	☐
… das Passiv mit '*by*' verwenden, wenn ich den 'Täter' oder 'Verursacher' der Handlung nennen will (z.B. *This picture was painted by Lowry*).	☐	☐	☐
… mit dem *past perfect* die Vorvergangenheit ausdrücken (z.B. *I couldn't pay because I had forgotten my money*).	☐	☐	☐
… in *indirect speech* berichten, was jemand sagt oder gesagt hat. Dabei verwende ich, wenn es nötig ist, andere Zeitformen und Pronomen (z.B. *Sam told Robert he had learnt a lot about boats*).	☐	☐	☐
VOKABELVERSTÄNDNIS: Ich kann …			
… Wörter für Sportarten, -plätze und -ausrüstung (z.B. *stadium, court, racket*) richtig verwenden.	☐	☐	☐
… einige Wörter, die als Verb und Nomen dieselbe Form haben (z.B. *sleep* = schlafen, *sleep* = Schlaf), richtig verwenden.	☐	☐	☐
… gebräuchliche Wörter und Wendungen für Diskussionen (z.B. *point of view, different views, agree/disagree*) richtig verwenden.	☐	☐	☐
… Wörter für die Freizeitaktivitäten von Teenagern (z.B. *cellphone, sleepover; hang out*) richtig verwenden.	☐	☐	☐
SKILLS – LERNEN UND ARBEITEN: Ich kann …			
… mit *brainstorming*-Techniken (*mind map, list,* 5 *Ws*) Ideen zu einem bestimmten Thema sammeln und ordnen.	☐	☐	☐
… Wörter für Personen, Gegenstände und Aktivitäten erklären, indem ich sie umschreibe. Dabei benutze ich z.B. einen Relativsatz oder die Wendungen *'It's like…, It's the opposite of…'*. Im Englischen nennt man dies *paraphrasing*.	☐	☐	☐

WAS ICH FÜR MEIN ENGLISCHLERNEN GETAN HABE: Ich habe …	**häufig**	**manchmal**	**nie**
… die Angaben im Grammar File in meinem Buch aufmerksam gelesen.	☐	☐	☐
… versucht, die Lern- und Arbeitstechniken im Skills File im Unterricht und bei den Hausaufgaben anzuwenden.	☐	☐	☐
… schon gelernte Vokabeln und Grammatik häufig aufgefrischt.	☐	☐	☐

WIE ICH MICH VERBESSERN KÖNNTE: Ich könnte …

- … im Unterricht aktiver mitarbeiten. ☐
- … ein zweiprachiges Wörterbuch häufiger verwenden. ☐
- … englische Internet-Seiten zu Unterrichtsthemen gezielt recherchieren. ☐
- … mir Texte auf meiner CD häufiger anhören. ☐
- … ein englisches *teen magazine* kaufen. ☐
- … eine/n englische/n e-pal suchen. ☐

Unit 5 A teen magazine

1 My teen mag ▸ pp. 94–95

a) *Look at pp. 94–95 of your student's book again. Teen magazines usually have articles on sports, music, films and fashion. Add more things that you often find there:*

You often find articles about celebrities (pop stars, film stars), ______________________

____

____

b) *If someone asked you to write an article for a teen magazine, would you write about sports, films, music or fashion? Say why.*

____

____

____

____

c) *What do you need for a video chat with friends? Write the words correctly.*

mweacb	rmoointr	imenrchpoo	seehnodahp	esomu
webcam	______	______	______	______

2 WORDS Through the alphabet with music ▸ p. 95

Complete the 'music words'.

A • Asian Fusion

B • ba______

C • ch______ • c____o • c______net

D • dr______ • D______

E • ele______c gu______

F • f____d____ • f____te

G • g______

H • h______ph______

I • (musical) i____str______

J • j____z

K • k______oa______

L • l______cs

M • m____i____l • mi______h____e

P • p____no • po______

R • r____p • r______hm • r______k

S • s____ph______ • s____ul • st______dr______

T • t____e • t____mb______ • tr______t

V • v______n

6402

3 STUDY SKILLS Skimming ▸ p. 96 • SF (p. 141)

a) *Skim the text and answer the questions below.*

And the winner is ...

About the show

It has different names in different countries, but it's the same all over the world. It's one of TV's most popular shows. If you think you can sing, if you want to become famous and maybe rich, if you want to meet celebrities and be everybody's favourite, then here's the show where you can try your luck.

Three or four celebrities listen, compare and say what they think about your singing. If you're good, you come back again next time. If you are not chosen, that's the end. You must leave the competition – and becoming a famous pop star will always be just a dream ...

What's 'The X Factor'?

It's that 'extra something' that makes a star. You have it – or you don't. Since the first show of this name in 2004 about 220,000 young people have tried their luck in the competition every year. The X Factor is the biggest TV talent competition in Europe. In the UK about 12.7 million people watch the final and choose their favourite.

In the final weeks before the winner is chosen, the ten best sing live before the nation. The winner records a single, which comes out just before Christmas. It usually becomes the Christmas Number One in the Top Ten charts. That's when a new star is born ...

Success – but for how long?

What happens to the winners? Do they really become stars for more than just a year? Do they really start a great job in pop music? And how much money do they really get? One thing is sure: their music managers and record companies get more – much more.

b) *What is the article about? Choose A, B or C.*

A a TV Top Ten show

B a TV music quiz show

C a TV talent competiton for pop singers

c) *What's the name of the German TV show that is the same?* ____________________

4 Which ones do you like best? (one/ones) ▸ p. 96

Latisha and her friend Nina are looking at teen magazines. Complete the dialogue with ***one*** *or* ***ones****.*

Info box

The first teenage magazine was published in the US in 1944. Its name was *Seventeen* and it's still successful.

Latisha What magazines do you like best? I like the *ones* with lots of star news. 'Bliss' is a good ________ . Oh, look. Here are two cool photos of Mika. I like the ________ on the right best. And there's another nice ________ here.

Nina Yes, they're great. He's a cool guy. Erm ... Which magazine has the best beauty tips?

Latisha Well, 'Cosmo Girl' usually has some interesting ________ . And problem pages?

Nina 'Sweet 16' and 'Sugar' have good ________ . And look at these two tops. I like the blue ________ best.

Latisha I like these trainers too. The pink and white ________ are great. Well, I know which magazine I'm going to buy – the cheapest ________ !

6504

5 What were they allowed to do? (have to and be allowed to)

▸ p. 97 • GF 12 (pp. 161–162)

*When they were at the music festival in Birmingham, Katrina and Latisha stayed at the girls' hostel. What were they (**not**) **allowed to do**? What did they (**not**) **have to do**?*

Were they allowed to …	Yes	No	**Did they have to …**	Yes	No
1 make breakfast in the kitchen?	✓		5 make their beds?		✓
2 make noise after 10 pm?		✓	6 share their room with other girls?	✓	
3 play music?	✓		7 clean their room?		✓
4 have showers after 10 pm?		✓	8 pay to use the internet?	✓	

1 *They were allowed to make breakfast in the kitchen.*

2 ______

3 ______

4 ______

5 *They didn't have to make their beds.*

6 ______

7 ______

6605 8 ______

6 Hassan wasn't able to go (be able to and be allowed to)

▸ p. 97 • GF 12 (pp. 161–162)

What are they saying? Choose the correct forms from the boxes to complete the speech bubbles.

1 Last week I *wasn't able to* go to band practice. Mum was angry with me, so I ______ go out. But everything at home is OK again now, so I ______ go next time.

'll be able to
wasn't able to
wasn't allowed to

2 I ______ use Dad's old headphones until my birthday. Then I ______ buy my own – I hope. But Dad ______ use my new ones!

won't be allowed to
'll be able to
'll be allowed to

3 I ______ write my article for the magazine next week because I'm staying with my aunt. I ______ play loud music there, but last time I ______ stay out late with my cousin.

was allowed to
won't be able to
won't be allowed to

6606

7 The Feely family (Reflexive pronouns)

▸ p. 98, p. 190 • GF 13 (pp. 162–163)

Mr and Mrs Feely have gone on a short holiday, so the Feely kids and Grandpa Feely have to look after themselves. Complete the sentences with:

myself • yourself • herself • itself • *ourselves* • yourselves • themselves

Tommy This week we have to cook for *ourselves*, Grandpa.

Grandpa But I can't cook for ____________ . You'll have to cook for me.

Tommy Grandpa, you can make ____________ some sandwiches. I'm going out now.

When Mum and Dad left, they said 'Enjoy ____________ '. Remember?

Grandpa Well, what about Jill and Jenny?

Tommy Don't worry about them, Grandpa. They can look after ____________ . They're at a sleepover.

Grandpa Oh. Well, can Mo cook for me?

Tommy Mo is in her room. She's teaching ____________ to play the violin. Can't you hear her?

Grandpa Oh, I thought that noise was the cat! Hmmm. And what about food?

Tommy Don't worry about the cat, Grandpa. The cat can feed ____________ .

6707 *Grandpa* Yes, I know that, but the cat can't feed me!

8 A real life story (Reflexive pronouns)

▸ p. 98, pp. 190, 192 • GF 13 (pp. 162–163)

Jimmy, a Canadian boy, sends in this 'real life' story to the editors of the teen magazine. Where do you need a reflexive pronoun?

I once stayed at a cabin by a lake with my dad. Before we left home my mom said: 'Look after *yourselves* and Jimmy, can you remember ____________ what to do if you see a bear? Take your knife with you.'

I don't like knives because I once cut ____________ badly, but I put it in my pocket. It's always very quiet in the forest, but that night it was windy. Around 12 o'clock I heard something outside. It was probably just the wind, but I felt ____________ scared. I imagined ____________ there was a bear at the door. When I'm scared, Dad always says 'Relax ____________ son. Don't worry ____________ about things that are only in your head.' But I wondered ____________ what the noise was, so I got ____________ dressed quickly. Something moved ____________ near the door. I looked through the window but it was too dark. Maybe it was hiding ____________ in the trees now. I didn't want Dad to get up, so I said to ____________ , 'Be a man! Take your knife and open the door!' But you can't teach ____________ to be a man.

I went back to bed, closed my eyes and put my MP3 headphones in my ears ...

6708 The next morning Dad said, 'Morning, son! I couldn't sleep last night, so I got up, went outside and walked around the cabin for a time. I hope you didn't hear me ...'

9 They understand each other (each other/themselves) ▸ p. 99 • GF 14 (pp. 163–164)

Look at the pictures. Then complete the sentences with ***each other*** *or* ***themselves****.*

1 

They understand *each other* .

2 

They've hurt ______________________ .

3 

They know ______________________ .

4 

They don't like ______________________ .

5 

6809 They're teaching ______________________ to cook.

6 

They're enjoying ______________________ .

Now you

How long have you and your best friend known each other? Why do you like each other? How do you help each other? Write a paragraph in your exercise book.

10 REVISION The video chat (Indirect speech) ▸ p. 99 • GF 11 (pp. 160–161)

Report what the four friends said at the video chat. Put the sentences into indirect speech.

1 We're making a magazine. I'm going to be the editor of the music section.

3 I need your articles in two weeks.

5 I've had a few ideas already.

2 I think I'll write about someone famous.

4 I already know what I'm going to write about.

6 I'll mail you the e-mail address.

1 Robert explained that *they were making a magazine. He was going to be the editor of the music section.*

2 Asif thought that ______________________ .

3 Robert explained that ______________________ .

4 Katrina said ______________________ .

5 Latisha said ______________________ .

6 Robert told them ______________________ .

11 Extra If Robert hadn't stayed ... (Conditional sentences 3)

▸ p. 99 • GF 15 (p. 164)

What would/wouldn't have happened if ...? Write conditional sentences and use the correct verb forms.

1 Robert stayed with family in Birmingham, so he went to the music festival.
If Robert *hadn't stayed with family in Birmingham,* *he wouldn't have gone to the music festival.*

2 He asked Asif about concert tickets. They became friends.
If he __________ Asif about concert tickets, they __________.

3 Robert didn't know what Asian Fusion was, so he asked Asif.
If Robert __________ what Asian Fusion was, __________.

4 The four teenagers liked each other, so they kept in touch.
If __________ __________.

5 Robert DJed at the centre, so the youth group asked him to be the music editor of their magazine.
__________ __________ __________

6911

12 REVISION Hassan's band (Adjective/Adverb)

▸ p. 99

Hassan's Asian Fusion band are practising a new song. But they aren't very happy with themselves. Complete the sentences with adjective or adverb forms.

Hassan Stop, stop, stop! That's *terrible* (terrible).
We're playing __________ (bad) today.
Last time we played quite __________ (good),
but this time it sounds __________ (awful).
The chorus should be __________ (fast).
We're still playing it too __________ (slow).
And Ali, play more __________ (careful).
You're making mistakes.

Ali I'm trying really __________ (hard), but
it's __________ (hard) to play
the chorus __________ (fast).

Hassan And play __________ (quiet) – or the neighbour will start to knock on the wall again.

Ali Maybe we should invite him to come and listen ... Maybe he'd like to join in!

13 WRITING COURSE Part 5: Correcting your text

▸ p. 99, p. 104/P 12 • SF (p. 147)

a) *Your friend's homework was: Write a short biography of a star. He/She wrote about Robbie Williams. Read the text carefully and mark the mistakes in red.*

Robbie Williams

Robbie Williams is born on 13 February, 1974, in Newcastle-under-Lyme, UK. His singing carreer started with the band Take That. He played with them for five years. The bands' success was huge. You could hear in the radio their songs. The others in the group said that Williams did not work hardly enough. He choosed to leave the band. In 1995 he has become a solo singer.

He released his first album in 1997. He has sold more then 50 million albums and 15 million singles too. In the UK he has sold more albums as any other solo singer in history. Williams has been popular all over the world. But he hasn't been so successful in North America. His best album in the US – 'Angels'– was only number 41 in the charts.

Info box

When Robbie Williams announced his World Tour for 2006, 1.6 million tickets were sold in one day! This gave Williams a place in the Guiness Book of Records!

7013

b) *There are ten mistakes. Where are they? Write the line numbers and correct the mistakes.*

	Mistake on line ...	Correct
Wrong spelling (2):	2	career
Wrong word:		
Wrong preposition:		
Wrong tense (2):		
Wrong irregular verb form:		
Wrong word order (SPO):		
Wrong adverb form:		
Wrong possessive form:		

c) **Extra** *How would you improve the text? Tick (✓) the boxes.*

I would ...

- use paragraphs. ☐
- use linking words (*and, so, but, when, although*). ☐
- add a few adverbs (*very, really*). ☐
- add time phrases (*every day, soon after that*). ☐

d) *In your exercise book, write the text again with your corrections from b) and your changes in c).*

14 WORDS Pairs

▸ p. 99

a) *Find and write pairs .*

disagree • *front* • begin • receive • agree • appear • forget • send • above • stop • mild • dry • spicy • below • *back* • wet • disappear • remember

front – *back* ______ – ______ ______ – ______

______ – ______ ______ – ______ ______ – ______

______ – ______ ______ – ______ ______ – ______

b) *Now choose a pair and use both words in one sentence.*

1 *Where do you sit in the classroom? At the front or at the back?*

2 ______

3 ______

4 ______

5 ______

7116 6 ______

15 Blue box: Nouns with -er or -or

▸ p. 99, p. 191

a) *Complete the words with the ending -er or -or.*

edit*or*	count______	direct______
elevat______	explor______	present______
invent______	dishwash______	murd______
support______	visit______	corn______
cook______	mirr______	leath______
collect______	murder______	monit______

b) *Now write the words in a) in two lists: people and things.*

People: *editor,* ______

______

______

Things: *counter,* ______

______

7115 ______

16 My book quiz ► p. 99

How well do you know your student's book?

***a)** Underline the right answer. The letters after your answers tell you if they are correct.*

1 The famous bridge in London that opens for ships is called …

London Bridge. (W)	Tower Bridge. (R)	Westminster Bridge. (C)

2 The names of the main Orkney Islands are Mainland, Flotta and …

Skye. (O)	Kirkwall. (R)	Hoy. (I)

3 L. S. Lowry was a famous …

footballer. (R)	writer. (O)	painter. (G)

4 Salford Quays is close to …

London. (G)	Edinburgh. (F)	Manchester. (H)

5 The capital of Canada is …

Ottawa. (T)	Toronto. (N)	Vancouver. (E)

***b)** On which pages can you find these sentences? Write the page numbers in the boxes.*

1 Bad timing for Latisha – she had a big football match on Saturday. ☐

2 A researcher was coming to interview some students for a TV documentary about the school. ☐

3 And then we change to the Jubilee Line. ☐

4 She was having a birthday party on Friday evening. ☐

Now add the page numbers together. If you get 179, your answers are correct.

***c)** Write answers (one word). Then write a letter from each answer.*

1 What's the name of Robert's friend who learns to paddle a boat? Sam (1) S

2 Which Caribbean island did Mrs Byrd's grandma come from? ________ (3) ___

3 In which town does Katrina go to school? ________ (7) ___

4 What's the name of the place where Asif likes to play video games? (London) ________ (1) ___

5 What's the name of the London borough where Asif lives? (Tower) ________ s (1) ___

6 What name did the 'Beauties' call Katrina? ________ (6) ___

7 What's the name of the film researcher who interviews Katrina? ________ (2) ___

► *Put the letters in the correct order to write the name of someone in your book:* ________ .

1 Complete the words.

Robert is going to be the ________r of the music ____t______ of their youth group's teen magazine.

You can send an article, and if it's interesting, they'll _____b_______ it. You can

send photos or d___________ too. If the magazine is a ___c__________, they'll

7301 do an e-zine too. Why don't you c __________ the centre's manager?

2 Rewrite this part with **one/ones**.

Asif wants to sell some CDs. He's got lots of old CDs that he doesn't need. Maybe he'll get enough money to buy a new CD.

____

7302 ____

3 Where must you add a reflexive pronoun (**myself, etc.**) or **each other**?

Can you imagine __________ a day without music? Music helps you to relax __________ .

It makes you feel __________ good. Teenagers usually love music, and they often teach __________ to play an instrument.

Robert taught __________ to DJ. Katrina would like to play the steel drum, and Latisha would like to

7303 play the fiddle. If Katrina lived in Manchester, or if Latisha lived on Hoy, they could teach __________ .

4 Complete with a form of **have to**, **be able to** or **be allowed to.**

1 I couldn't speak English five years ago, but I ________________ speak it well when I leave school.

2 Latisha couldn't go out last night because she ______________ do lots of homework.

3 Robert ____________________ stay out late a few years ago, but now he sometimes stays out until 11 pm.

4 Asif has lost his mobile. He _______________ buy a new one with his birthday money next week.

5 Asif's dad is going to buy a new computer, but he says Asif ________________________ use it.

7304 *6* Robert was ill yesterday so he ________________________ DJ at the community hall.

20 points

Now you

If you were the editor of a teen magazine, what kind of sections, articles, photos and stories would you put in? Say why. Write two or three paragraphs in your exercise book.

7305
7306 *If I were the editor of a teen magazine, I would ...*

- Hier kannst du deine Antworten im Checkpoint überprüfen. Falls du Probleme mit den jeweiligen Aufgaben hattest, folge den Lernhilfen in der rechten Spalte. Die Verweise beziehen sich auf dein Schülerbuch.
- Deine Punktzahl kannst du ermitteln, indem du dir für jede richtige Lösung einen Punkt gibst. Schreib deine Gesamtpunktzahl in das gelbe Kästchen unten links.

1 Transport: What is it?

1 a ferry
2 a tram
3 a platform
4 a ticket machine
5 a bus stop
6 an airport

6 P.

- Schau dir im Skills File in deinem Buch den Punkt zu *Learning words* (S. 133–134) an.
- Lern die Wörter mithilfe des Vocabulary (*Word field: Transport*, S. 173) und der Übung 1 im Practice-Teil deines Buchs (S. 20).

2 Have you ever ...?

Asif Have you ever eaten
Robert ate
Have you ever tried
Robert 've eaten/have eaten
Asif did you have
Robert had

6 P.

- Lies dir Grammar File 1 zum *present perfect* und *simple past* durch (S. 149).
- Löse die Aufgabe 5 im Practice-Teil (S. 21).

3 Since or for?

3 P.

1 for 2 since 3 for

- Den richtigen Gebrauch von *since* und *for* erklärt dir das Grammar File 2 (S. 150).
- Üben kannst du das *present perfect* mit *since* und *for*, indem du die Aufgabe 7 im Practice-Teil noch einmal löst (S. 22).

4 Underline the correct verb form.

1 (been knowing/known).
2 (have been walking/have walked)
3 (has had/has been having)

3 P.

- Wie du das *present perfect simple* und das *present perfect progressive* verwendest, erfährst du in den Grammar Files 1b (S. 149) und 3 (S. 151).
- Wiederhole die Aufgaben 9 und 10 im Practice-Teil (S. 23).

Now you (Ideas)

take a bus tour/see sights/walk through Hyde Park/ see Buckingham Palace/take photos/buy sandwiches for lunch/great weather/ask the way/take the Tube/ visit Tower of London/see Gherkin and St Paul's/eat at a Bangladeshi restaurant/next day/go on the Eye/ fantastic views of London/visit Science Museum/see Stephenson's Rocket/go to Covent Garden/see street performers/very tired/go to bed early

- Um Ideen über London zu sammeln, kannst du dir die Unit 1 in deinem Buch noch einmal anschauen oder auch im Internet recherchieren.
- Schau im Skills File (S. 146) nach, wie du deine Ideen sammeln und ordnen und deine Sätze interessanter gestalten kannst.
- Die Übung 11 im Practice-Teil (S. 24) zeigt dir noch einmal, wie du deinen Schreibstil verbessern kannst.

Ich habe ☐ Punkte von 18.

18–16	Sehr gut. Weiter so!
15–13	Schon recht gut.
Unter 13	Genauer lernen!

1 Town and country: Write the words.

1 coast
4 bay
2 shopping precinct
5 car park
3 salmon
6 scenery

6 P.

Falls du Probleme hattest:

- Wie du Wörter besser lernen kannst und worauf du achten musst, erfährst du im Skills File auf den S. 133–134.
- Diese Wörter findest du im Vocabulary auf den S. 176 und 178.

2 If I had more pocket money, …

Leo	had	
Marie	would spend	
Leo	got	would save
Marie	wanted	would find
Leo	worked	would have to

8P.

- Im Grammar File 6 (S. 153–154) erfährst du, wie du Bedingungssätze (Typ 2) bildest.
- Wiederhole die Aufgaben 10a/b und 11a im Practice-Teil (S. 42).

3 Computers and mobiles

Leo likes to chat to his friends on his computer after school. It's cheaper than phone calls.

He likes to surf the internet too. It's more fun than homework.

Marie likes to send text messages to her friends on her mobile. She thinks it's more fun than instant messages on the computer.

She has a cool logo on her mobile, a picture of her cat, Tabby. And guess what her ringtone is – Tabby too!

6 P.

- Informationen über elektronische Medien bekommst du auf den S. 32 und 176 in deinem Buch.

Now you (Ideas)

go to Kirkwall/see Katrina's school/walk along the coast to see the Old Man of Hoy/take photos/visit a salmon farm/see Flotta's oil terminal/visit the island shop/take a bus tour of Edinburgh/see the sights/visit Edinburgh Castle/go shopping in Princes Street/take photos/go to a tea shop/eat Scottish shortbread/try haggis/listen to the bagpipes/ take photos of Loch Ness/look for Nessie/buy a book about Loch Ness and the Monster/stay the night at a Scottish castle

- Schau dir die Unit 2 in deinem Buch noch einmal an, um Informationen über Schottland zu sammeln.
- Wie du deinen Text gut strukturieren kannst, zeigt dir die Übung 4 im Practice-Teil (S. 39).
- Im Skills File (S. 146) erfährst du mehr zum Thema *using paragraphs.*

Ich habe ______ Punkte von 20.

20–18	Sehr gut. Weiter so!
17–14	Schon recht gut.
Unter 14	Genauer lernen!

1 What are they? Write the names.

1 goalkeeper
2 running track
3 coach
4 table tennis bat
5 swimsuit
6 sledge

6 P.

Falls du Probleme hattest:

- Schau dir im Skills File den Punkt zu *Learning words* (S. 133–134) noch einmal an.
- Lern die Wörter mithilfe des Vocabulary (S. 181–184).

2 Paraphrasing

1 Galerie:
It's a place that shows paintings and interesting art.

2 Gymnastikanzug:
It's something girls wear for jazz dance.

3 Torwart:
It's the player who stops the ball in the goal.

3 P.

- Im Skills File (S. 144) erfährst du, wie du am besten beim *paraphrasing* vorgehst.
- Lies dir auch das Grammar File 7 (S. 154–156) zu den Relativsätzen durch.
- Schau dir die Übungen 3a (S. 63) und 3b (S. 111) im Practice-Teil noch einmal an und umschreibe die Wörter in den grünen Kästen.

3 Complete with the passive.

1 The Lowry Centre was opened (open) in 2000.
2 The Lowry is named (name) after a famous painter.
3 Lots of Lowry's paintings are shown (show) in the galleries.
4 Manchester's oldest buildings were built (build) in the 15th century.

4 P.

- Im Grammar File 8 (S. 156–157) erfährst du, wie du das Passiv formst und verwendest.
- Üben kannst du das Passiv, indem du die Aufgaben 8 und 9 im Practice-Teil (S. 65) wiederholst.

4 Complete the text.

Rosehill beat St. Joseph's in the schools' football cup final in Bridgeford last Saturday. At half-time the score was 0–1 for St. Joseph's. After the break. Rosehill's captain Nick Scott was fouled by St. Joseph's captain. He took the penalty and scored his second goal in the 89th minute.

7 P.

- Schau dir die S. 56 und 180–181 in deinem Buch noch einmal an, um die 'Sport'-Wörter zu wiederholen.

Now you (Ideas)

would like to see Old Trafford/famous football stadium/very interesting for football fans/visit Salford Quays/take photos/visit the Lowry/good if you are interested in modern art/see Lowry's paintings/go to other museums/learn about the history of the city

- Suche in Unit 3 oder im Internet nach interessanten Informationen über Manchester.
- Schau dir im Skills File die S. 146 an, um deinen Text besser strukturieren zu können.

Ich habe ______ Punkte von 20.

20–18	Sehr gut. Weiter so!
17–14	Schon recht gut.
Unter 14	Genauer lernen!

1 Complete the words.

1 p opulation
2 F irst Nations
3 h unt
4 w eigh
5 p addle

5 P.

2 Underline the correct verb form.

1 (were/had been) (had stopped/stopped)
2 (caught/had caught)
3 (broke/had broken)
4 (just reached/had just reached)
(had seen/saw)

6 P.

3 More words: What's missing?

1 adults
2 strict
3 volunteer
4 local
5 malls/precincts

5 P.

4 What did Robert tell Sam after the party?

1 Robert said (that) everyone had really enjoyed the party.
2 He told Sam (that) Jessica wanted him to DJ at her party.
3 He said (that) they were driving up to the cabin soon.
4 He told Sam (that) he would call again when they got home.

4 P.

Now you (Ideas)

would like to visit the cities Toronto, Vancouver, Montréal/see the sights/take photos/learn about the history of Canada/stay at a cabin/see bears/ learn how to protect yourself from bears/ talk to First Nations people/visit some national parks/ paddle a canoe/see a dragon boat race/go to the Niagara Falls

Ich habe ______ Punkte von 20.

20–18 Sehr gut. Weiter so!
17–14 Schon recht gut.
Unter 14 Genauer lernen!

Falls du Probleme hattest:

- Lies dir im Skills File die S. 133–134 noch einmal durch.
- Lern die Wörter mithilfe des Vocabulary (S. 185–187).

- Wie du das *past perfect* und das *simple past* verwendest, kannst du in den Grammar Files 9 und 10a (S. 158–159) nachlesen.
- Wiederhole die Übungen 4 und 5 im Practice-Teil (S. 81).

- Schau dir die S. 74 und 185–186 noch einmal an, um die Wörter zu lernen.

- Im Grammar File 11 (S. 160–161) erfährst du das Wichtigste zum *indirect speech*.
- Löse die Aufgaben 9–10 (S. 83) und 12 (S. 84) im Practice-Teil.

- Durchsuche die Unit 4 nach interessanten Dingen zu Kanada.
- Schau dir im Practice-Teil die Übung 13 (S. 85) noch einmal an, um zu erfahren, wie du einen interessanten Text schreiben kannst.
- Auch das Skills File (S. 146) kann dir behilflich sein.

1 Complete the words.

Robert is going to be the editor of the music section of their youth group's teen magazine. You can send an article, and if it's interesting, they'll publish it. You can send photos or drawings too. If the magazine is a success, they'll do an e-zine too. Why don't you contact the centre's manager?

6 P.

2 Rewrite this part with one/ones.

Asif wants to sell some CDs. He's got lots of old ones that he doesn't need. Maybe he'll get enough money to buy a new one.

2 P.

3 Where must you add a reflexive pronoun (myself, etc.) or each other?

–	–
–	themselves
himself	each other

6 P.

4 Complete with a form of have to, be able to or be allowed to.

1 will be able to
2 had to
3 wasn't allowed to
4 will have to
5 won't be allowed to
6 wasn't able to

6 P.

Now you (Ideas)

articles about famous people/because teenagers who buy teenage magazines like to read about their favourite pop stars, film stars/interesting photos of bands, sports events, stars/interviews with celebrities/tips about new films, new books, new computer games/section on fashion/problem page/interesting web links/useful web addresses/real life stories from readers/letters from readers/quizzes/competitions

Ich habe ______ Punkte von 20.

20–18 Sehr gut. Weiter so!
17–14 Schon recht gut.
Unter 14 Genauer lernen!

Falls du Probleme hattest:

- Lern die Wörter mithilfe des Vocabulary (S. 189).

- Wiederhole die Übung 3a im Practice-Teil (S. 101).

- Wie du *reflexive pronouns* und *each other* verwendest, kannst du in den Grammar Files 13 und 14 (S. 162–163) nachlesen.
- Schau dir dazu auch im Vocabulary die blauen Kästen auf den S. 190 und 192 an.
- Löse die Aufgaben 6 und 7 im Practice-Teil (S. 102).

- Das Grammar File 12 (S. 161–162) zeigt dir, wie du die modalen Ersatzverben einsetzen kannst.
- Wiederhole die Übungen 4a und 5 (S. 101) im Practice-Teil.

- Um Ideen zu sammeln, kannst du dir die Unit 5 noch einmal anschauen.
- In der Übung 12a im Practice-Teil (S. 104) erfährst du, wie du deinen Text überprüfen und korrigieren kannst.
- Im Skills File ist auf den S. 146–147 alles zusammengefasst, was du wissen musst, um einen interessanten Text zu schreiben.

Unit 1

GF 1 The present perfect and the simple past in contrast ▸ *GF p. 149*

a) REVISION The simple past

Last weekend Robert **went** to London with his parents.

Asif **met** them at the London Eye and they all **had** a great time.

On Sunday they **visited** the Tower,
and then they **took** the Tube to Waterloo.

Mit dem ***simple past*** berichtest du über Vergangenes – z. B., wenn du eine Geschichte erzählst.
Das *simple past* drückt aus, dass etwas zu einem **bestimmten Zeitpunkt** oder **in einem bestimmten abgeschlossenen Zeitraum** in der Vergangenheit geschah. (Frage: **Wann?**)
Daher findest du in *simple past*-Sätzen oft **genaue Zeitangaben** wie *last weekend, yesterday, a week ago.*

b) REVISION The present perfect

Asif **has** already **visited** the London Trocadero.
... hat schon mal ... besucht

He **has** always **wanted** to go on the London Eye, but he **hasn't done** that yet.
... hat schon immer ... gehen wollen
... hat ... noch nicht getan

He and his friends **have** often **been** to Brick Lane Market.
... sind schon oft ... gewesen

Mit dem ***present perfect*** drückst du aus, dass etwas **irgendwann in der Vergangenheit** geschehen ist.
Daher findest du oft **Adverbien der unbestimmten Zeit** in *present perfect*-Sätzen, z. B.

already	schon (mal)	*always*	(schon) immer
just	gerade (eben)	*never*	(noch) nie
not ... yet	noch nicht	*often*	(schon) oft
ever?	jemals?	*yet?*	schon?

! Beim ***present perfect*** ist der genaue Zeitpunkt des Geschehens nicht wichtig oder nicht bekannt.

c) Present perfect or simple past?

◂ 1 Asif fragt, ob Robert **überhaupt schon mal** türkisch gegessen hat – also ***present perfect***:

***Have** you ever **tried** Turkish food?*

◂ 2 Dann möchte er wissen, **wann** das war, und er fragt daher im ***simple past***:

*And when **did** you **try** it?*

◂ 3 Robert antwortet im ***simple past***, weil er den **genauen Zeitpunkt** nennt:

*We **went** to a Turkish restaurant last Saturday.*

Unit 2

GF 2 The present perfect with since and for ▸ *GF p. 150*

Du kannst das *present perfect* verwenden, um über einen **Zustand** zu sprechen, der in der Vergangenheit begonnen hat und jetzt noch andauert.

Oft findest du dabei Zeitangaben mit ***since*** oder ***for***:

1 Robert and his parents **have been** in England since September 1st.
Robert und seine Eltern **sind** seit dem 1. September in England.

2 Robert and his parents **have been** in England for ten days.
Robert und seine Eltern **sind** seit zehn Tagen in England.

◂ 1 Mit ***since*** („seit") gibst du einen **Zeitpunkt** an *(since September 1st; since 2006; since 12 o'clock)*.
since **+ Zeitpunkt** drückt also aus, **seit wann** ein Zustand andauert.

◂ 2 Mit ***for*** („seit") gibst du einen **Zeitraum** an *(for ten days; for years; for a long time)*.
for **+ Zeitraum** drückt also aus, **wie lange** ein Zustand bereits andauert.

Robert has known Asif since the music festival.
Robert kennt Asif seit dem Musikfestival.
But he feels like he has known him for years.
..., als ob er ihn seit Jahren kennt.

How long **have** you **lived** in this part of town?
– Since last month. / For a few weeks.
Wie lange **wohnt** ihr in diesem Teil der Stadt?
– Seit letztem Monat. / Seit ein paar Wochen.

! Achtung:
Im **Deutschen** benutzt man meist das **Präsens**:
*Er **kennt** ihn seit ...*
Im **Englischen** muss das ***present perfect*** stehen:
*He **has known** him since/for ...*

Mit ***How long ...?*** + *present perfect* kannst du fragen, seit wann oder wie lange ein Zustand schon andauert.

GF 3 The present perfect progressive ▸ *GF p. 151*

a) Use

Robert I'**ve been watching** the acrobat for a few minutes.
Ich **schaue** seit einigen Minuten dem Akrobaten zu.

Mr Smith And we'**ve been walking** around since lunchtime.
Und wir **laufen** seit Mittag umher.

Mit dem *present perfect progressive* kannst du ausdrücken, dass eine **Handlung** oder ein **Vorgang** in der Vergangenheit begonnen hat und bis jetzt andauert.

Zeitangaben mit ***since*** und ***for*** werden genauso verwendet wie bei der einfachen Form des *present perfect*:

since **+ Zeitpunkt (seit wann?)**
for **+ Zeitraum (wie lange?)**

! Auch in diesen Fällen benutzt man im **Deutschen** meist das **Präsens**:
*Wir **laufen** umher seit ...*
Im **Englischen** steht das ***present perfect progressive***:
*We'**ve been walking** around since/for ...*

b) Form

Present perfect progressive

Statements

+	I/You/We/They	**have been waiting**
	He/She/It	**has been waiting**
–	I/You/We/They	**haven't been waiting**
	He/She/It	**hasn't been waiting**

Questions

Have you **been waiting** long?
Has she **been waiting** long?

How long **have** you **been waiting**?
How long **has** she **been waiting**?

What **have** you **been doing**?
Who **has** Robert **been watching**?

Das *present perfect progressive* bildest du mit ***have/has been*** + ***ing*-Form**.

Unit 2

GF 4 Talking about the future ▸ *GF p. 152*

a) The *going to*-future

Jane, a researcher, **is going to interview** some students for a TV documentary.
Jane ... hat vor/plant, einige Schüler und Schülerinnen ... zu interviewen.

Wie du weißt, benutzt du das Futur mit ***am/are/is going to*** **+ Infinitiv**, wenn du über **Vorhaben** und **Pläne** für die Zukunft sprechen willst.

Mit ***going to*** **+ Infinitiv** kannst du auch ausdrücken, dass etwas **wahrscheinlich gleich passieren** wird.
Es gibt dafür schon deutliche **Anzeichen** (hier: das Kabel, das sich um das Bein des Assistenten gewickelt hat).

b) The *will*-future

Maybe Katrina **will talk** about the school band.
Vielleicht wird Katrina über die Schülerband sprechen.

Katrina **will be** 14 next year.
Katrina wird nächstes Jahr 14.

Mit ***will/won't* + Infinitiv** kannst du Vermutungen und Vorhersagen über die Zukunft äußern.

◂ Eine **Vermutung** fängt oft mit *I think, I'm sure* oder *maybe* an.

◂ Bei einer **Vorhersage** geht es oft um Dinge, die man nicht beeinflussen kann, z.B. das Wetter oder das Alter.

c) The present progressive with future meaning

Katrina's mum Your dad **is picking** you up from school on Friday.
Dein Vater holt dich am Freitag von der Schule ab. / ... wird dich ... abholen.

Katrina What **are** you **doing** on Friday? Why **aren't** you **coming**?
Was machst du am Freitag? Warum kommst du nicht?

Feste Pläne und **Verabredungen** kannst du auch mit dem *present progressive* ausdrücken. Dabei muss klar sein, dass es sich um etwas Zukünftiges handelt, z.B. durch eine Zeitangabe wie *on Friday, next week, at the weekend, tomorrow*.
(Manchmal wird diese Verwendung des *present progressive* auch ***diary future***, deutsch „Kalender-Zukunft", genannt, weil es sich um Verabredungen handelt, die man schon in seinen Terminkalender eingetragen hat.)

GF 5 The *will*-future for spontaneous decisions ▸ *GF p. 153*

Alison Which bags do you mean, Fiona?

Linda The bags from the magazine.
I'll show you ... here, look.
... Ich zeig sie dir ... hier, schau.

I'm thirsty. – I'**ll get** you a drink.
(Angebot)

What a lot of work! – I'**ll help** you. I promise.
(Versprechen)

Das *will-future* verwendest du auch, wenn du einen spontanen (nicht geplanten) Entschluss fasst.
Oft handelt es sich dabei um Hilfsangebote oder Versprechen.

! Im Deutschen steht bei einem spontanen Entschluss meist die Gegenwart. Im Englischen muss das *will-future* stehen:

I'll show you ...
Ich zeig sie dir ...

GF 6 Conditional sentences (type 2) ▸ *GF pp. 153–154*

a) REVISION Conditional sentences (type 1)

Alison If they **choose** you, you'**ll be** a star.
Wenn sie dich wählen, bist du ... /
Wenn sie dich wählen, wirst du ... sein.

Linda If **I don't get** to the shop soon, they **won't have** those trendy new bags any more.

Du kennst bereits Bedingungssätze vom Typ 1 (**„Was <u>ist</u>, wenn ..."-Sätze**).
Sie sagen aus, was unter bestimmten Bedingungen geschieht oder nicht geschieht:

***if*-Satz (Bedingung)**	**Hauptsatz (Folge)**
*If they **choose** you,*	*you'**ll be** a star.*
simple present	***will-future***

b) Conditional sentences (type 2)

Wenn mich ein Filmemacher entdecken würde, wäre ich berühmt / würde ich berühmt.

Ich würde nicht hier wohnen, wenn ich reich und berühmt wäre.

Bedingungssätze vom Typ 2 sind **„Was <u>wäre</u>, wenn ..."-Sätze**.
Sie drücken aus, was unter bestimmten Bedingungen **sein würde**, aber doch eher unwahrscheinlich ist (oder sogar unmöglich):

Es ist unwahrscheinlich, dass Fiona von einem Filmemacher entdeckt werden wird. Also wird sie wahrscheinlich auch nicht berühmt.

***if*-Satz (Bedingung)**	**Hauptsatz (Folge)**
*If a film-maker **discovered** me,*	*I **would be** famous.*
simple past	***would + infinitive***

(Kurzform von *I/you/he/... would: I'd / you'd / he'd / ...*)

If a film-maker **discovered** me, ...
Wenn mich ein Filmemacher entdecken würde, ...

If I **had** enough money, I could **buy** a new bike.
Wenn ich genug Geld hätte, könnte ich mir ein neues Rad kaufen.

! Im *if*-Satz steht **kein *would***.
Also nicht: *If a film-maker ~~would discover~~ me, ...*

Im Hauptsatz kann auch *could* („könnte") stehen.

Unit 3

GF 7 Relative clauses ▸ *GF pp. 154–157*

a) REVISION Relative pronouns

Mit Relativsätzen sagst du genauer, wen oder was du meinst.

The **girl** who plays for United U14s is Latisha.
Das Mädchen, das für die U14 von *United* spielt, ...

Asif is **a boy** who Latisha knows from the festival in Birmingham.
... ein Junge, den Latisha vom Festival ... kennt.

◂ In Relativsätzen, die **Personen** beschreiben, verwendest du ***who***:
the man / the woman / people *who* ...
der Mann, der ... / die Frau, die ... / Leute, die ...

Do you know **a shop** which sells cheap CDs?
... einen Laden, der billige CDs verkauft?

Mrs Byrd has cooked **a dish** which Anna likes.
... ein Gericht, das Anna mag.

◂ In Relativsätzen, die **Dinge** (und Tiere) beschreiben, verwendest du ***which***:
the shop / the dish / an animal *which* ...
der Laden, der ... / das Gericht, das ... / ein Tier, das ...

... **the friends** that Latisha met at the festival
... **a shop** that sells cheap CDs

◂ Das Relativpronomen ***that*** wird für Personen und Dinge verwendet.

The girl **who plays** football ...
Das Mädchen, **das** Fußball **spielt** ...

! Beachte die unterschiedliche Wortstellung in englischen und deutschen Relativsätzen.

b) Contact clauses

Das Relativpronomen kann **Subjekt** oder **Objekt** sein.

1 Anna is a girl **who** is staying with the Byrds.
..., **das** bei den Byrds wohnt.

1 Das Relativpronomen ist **Subjekt des Relativsatzes** (es steht direkt vor dem Verb):

	Subjekt	
Anna is a girl	***who***	*is staying with the Byrds.*
Anna ist ein Mädchen,	***das***	*bei den Byrds wohnt.*
Plantains are bananas	***that***	*grow in Trinidad.*
Plantains sind Bananen,	***die***	*auf Trinidad wachsen.*

2 Beckham is the only player who Anna knows.
..., den Anna kennt.

2 Das Relativpronomen ist Objekt **des Relativsatzes**:

	Objekt	Subjekt	
Beckham is the only player	*who*	*Anna*	*knows.*
Beckham ist der einzige Spieler,	*den*	*Anna*	*kennt.*
Football is a sport	*that*	*Latisha*	*loves.*
Fußball ist ein Sport,	*den*	*Latisha*	*liebt.*

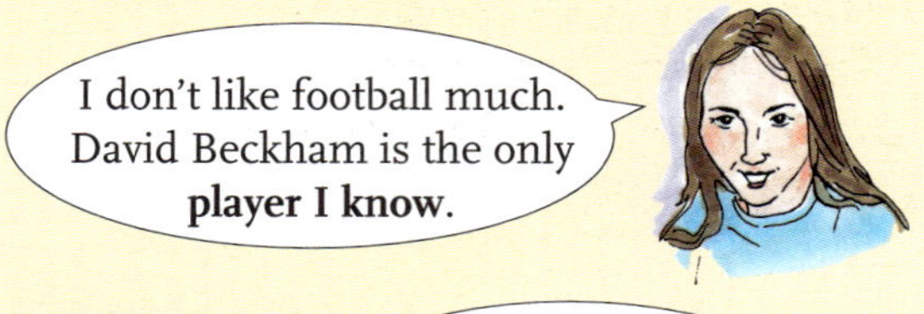

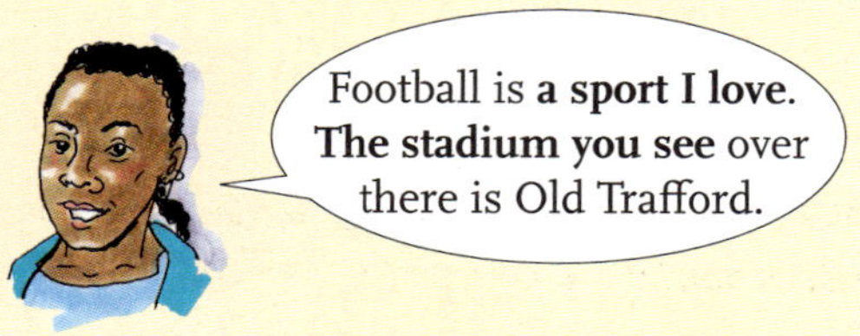

◂ Wenn das Relativpronomen **Objekt** des Relativsatzes ist, wird es manchmal **weggelassen** – wie in den Beispielen links. Relativsätze ohne Relativpronomen nennt man *contact clauses*.

Mrs Byrd is somebody who likes cooking.
(*not:* Mrs Byrd is ~~somebody likes cooking~~.)

! Achtung:
Wenn das **Relativpronomen direkt vor dem Verb** steht, ist es Subjekt – dann darfst du es **nicht weglassen**!

The girl **Latisha is chatting** with is Katrina.
Das Mädchen, mit dem Latisha chattet, ist Katrina.

The stadium **they are looking** at is Old Trafford.

! Beachte die Stellung der Präposition in Relativsätzen mit Verben wie *talk to, chat with, look at, stay with*.
Die Präposition steht an derselben Stelle wie im Hauptsatz.

GF 8 The passive ▸ *GF pp. 156–157*

a) Active and passive

Active: Kids play football all over the world.

Mit einem **Aktivsatz** drückst du aus, **wer oder was etwas tut**. Das Subjekt des Aktivsatzes führt die Handlung aus:

Subjekt	**Verb** (aktiv)	**Objekt**	**...**
Kids	*play*	*football*	...
Jugendliche	*spielen*	*Fußball*	...

Passive: Football is played all over the world.
Fußball wird überall auf der Welt gespielt.

Mit einem **Passivsatz** drückst du aus, **mit wem oder womit etwas geschieht**. Das Objekt des Aktivsatzes *(football)* wird Subjekt des Passivsatzes:

Subjekt	**Verb** (passiv)	**...**
Football	*is played*	...
Fußball	*wird gespielt*	...

b) Form

... ist nach einem berühmten Maler ... benannt.
... wurde im Jahr 2000 eröffnet.
Viele Gemälde werden ... ausgestellt/gezeigt.

Das Passiv bildest du mit einer **Form von *be*** und der 3. Form des Verbs. Die 3. Form des Verbs heißt **Partizip Perfekt** *(past participle)*.

Simple present: *am/are/is* **+ *past participle***
*The Lowry is **named** ...*
*Lowry's paintings are **shown** ...*

Simple past: *was/were* **+ *past participle***
*The Lowry was **opened** ...*

c) Use

At 8.45 yesterday morning a 12-year-old boy was hurt in a car accident on Duke Street. The police were called and the boy was taken to hospital.

Mit einem Passivsatz kannst du Handlungen beschreiben, ohne zu sagen, wer die Handlung ausführt. Oft ist gar nicht bekannt oder nicht wichtig, wer die Handlung ausführt.
Du findest daher das Passiv oft in Nachrichten und in Zeitungsberichten (z.B. über Unfälle, Verbrechen) oder auf Schildern.

Ein englischer Passivsatz wird im Deutschen oft durch einen Aktivsatz mit „man" wiedergegeben:
*The boy **was taken** to hospital.*
***Man brachte** den Jungen ins Krankenhaus.*

d) Passive sentences with *by* ...

The planet Uranus **was discovered** by William Herschel in 1781.
... wurde 1781 von William Herschel entdeckt.

My parents' house **was destroyed** by fire.
... wurde durch ein Feuer zerstört.

Wenn du in einem Passivsatz den „Täter" oder „Verursacher" nennen willst, verwendest du die Präposition ***by*** („von", „durch").

Unit 4

GF 9 The past perfect ▸ *GF p. 158*

a) Use

After school Robert **went** to the mall. ... ging ...
He **wanted** to buy a birthday present. ... wollte ...

◂ Du benutzt das *simple past* für **Handlungen, Ereignisse und Zustände in der Vergangenheit**.

Robert went to the mall because he had planned to meet Sam there.
..., weil er ausgemacht hatte, Sam dort zu treffen.

Robert had already chosen a present when Sam came in.
Robert hatte bereits ein Geschenk ausgesucht, ...

◂ Mit dem ***past perfect*** (Plusquamperfekt, Vorvergangenheit) drückst du aus, dass eine Handlung noch **vor einer anderen Handlung in der Vergangenheit** stattgefunden hatte. Die Handlung im *past perfect* geschah zuerst:

2	1
*Robert **went** to the mall*	*because he had planned to ...*

1	2
He had already chosen a present	*when Sam **came** in.*

Past perfect
When Sam arrived, Robert had bought a DVD for Ashley.
Als Sam eintraf, hatte Robert (bereits) eine DVD für Ashley gekauft. *(der Kauf geschah vor Sams Eintreffen)*

Simple past
When Sam arrived, Robert bought a DVD for Ashley.
Als Sam eintraf, kaufte Robert eine DVD für Ashley. *(der Kauf geschah erst nach Sams Eintreffen)*

! Beachte die Bedeutungsunterschiede zwischen *past perfect* und *simple past*.

b) Form

Robert knew where there was a big DVD shop because he'd been there before.
..., weil er schon einmal dort gewesen war.

Das *past perfect* bildest du mit ***had*** (Kurzform: *'d*) und der 3. Form des Verbs. Die 3. Form des Verbs heißt **Partizip Perfekt** *(past participle)*.

Had he bought the present when Sam arrived? Hatte er das Geschenk schon gekauft, ...?

! Beim *past perfect* must du immer ***had*** verwenden, egal ob im Deutschen „hatte" oder „war" steht.

GF 11 Indirect speech ▸ *GF pp. 160–161*

a) Direct and indirect speech

Das, was jemand sagt (oder gesagt hat), kannst du direkt oder indirekt wiedergeben.

Direct speech Ashley says, 'I love Nickelback!'
Ashley sagt: „Ich liebe Nickelback!"

◂ In der **direkten Rede** *(direct speech)* gibst du **wörtlich** wieder, was jemand sagt oder schreibt.
Direkte Rede steht in der Regel in Anführungszeichen.

Indirect speech Ashley **says** (that) she loves Nickelback.
Ashley sagt, dass sie Nickelback liebt.

◂ In der **indirekten Rede** (*indirect speech* oder *reported speech*) berichtest du, was jemand sagt oder schreibt.
Die indirekte Rede wird mit Verben wie *say, tell sb., answer, explain, write* eingeleitet.

! Im Englischen steht vor der indirekten Rede **kein Komma**.
Das Wort *that* wird oft weggelassen.

b) Indirect speech: tense changes

Wenn das einleitende Verb im ***simple past*** steht (*she **said**, he **wrote*** usw.), werden in der indirekten Rede meist andere Zeitformen verwendet als in der direkten Rede:

Tense changes

	Direct speech	Indirect speech
present ▸ past	*Ashley* 'I'm not sure.' 'I'm waiting for Robert.'	Ashley **said** she wasn't sure. Ashley **said** she was waiting for Robert.
past ▸ past perfect	*Robert* 'It was a great party.'	Robert **told** Sam it had been a great party.
present perfect ▸ past perfect	*Robert* 'I haven't called Emily.'	Robert **told** Sam he hadn't called Emily.
***will*-future ▸ *would* + infinitive**	*Sam* 'I'll call Ashley.'	Sam **said** he would call Ashley.
***going to*-future ▸ *was/were going to* + infinitive**	*Sam* 'I'm going to practise paddling.'	Sam **said** he was going to practise paddling.

– Verben im *past perfect* bleiben unverändert, da man sie nicht weiter „zurückverschieben" kann.
– In der Umgangssprache werden *simple past*-Formen der direkten Rede oft nicht ins *past perfect* verändert.

c) Indirect speech: changes of pronouns

Robert 'Sam, **I**'ll call **you** when **we**'re back.'
„Sam, ich rufe dich an, wenn wir zurück sind."

Wie im Deutschen hängt die Veränderung der Pronomen in der indirekten Rede davon ab, wer wem berichtet.

Unit 5

GF 12 Modals and their substitutes ▸ *GF pp. 161–162*

a) REVISION *can – may – must*

Latisha can play football very well.
Can/May I go to the match, Mum?
Latisha must do her homework first.

Can, may und ***must*** sind modale Hilfsverben (*modal auxiliaries* oder kurz: *modals*). Sie drücken aus, dass jemand etwas tun **kann, darf** oder **muss**.

b) (to) be able to – (to) be allowed to – (to) have to

Wenn es um „können/dürfen/müssen" in der Vergangenheit oder der Zukunft geht, werden meist **Ersatzverben** verwendet:

„können": *(to) be able to*
- **Vergangenheit** (wenn jemand etwas tun **konnte**): ***was/were able to***
- **Zukunft** (wenn jemand etwas tun **können wird**): ***will be able to***

Jack was ill on Friday, but he was able to **go** to the disco on Saturday. ... konnte gehen ...

Holly didn't have much time yesterday, but she will be able to **buy** a present for her dad tomorrow. ... wird kaufen können ...

„dürfen": *(to) be allowed to*
- **Vergangenheit** (wenn jemand etwas tun **durfte**): ***was/were allowed to***
- **Zukunft** (wenn jemand etwas tun **dürfen wird**): ***will be allowed to***

Jodie wasn't allowed to **go** to the school disco last month. ... durfte nicht gehen ...

She won't be allowed to **go** to Lauren's party on Saturday. ... wird nicht gehen dürfen...

Holly had to **clean** her room yesterday.
... musste putzen ...

She can go to the party, but she will have to **be** home by ten.
... wird sein müssen ...

„müssen“: *(to) have to*
- **Vergangenheit** (wenn jemand etwas tun **musste**): ***had to***
- **Zukunft** (wenn jemand etwas tun **müssen wird**): ***will have to***

I could **hear** music, but I couldn't **see** anybody.

Zu *can* gibt es auch die Vergangenheitsform *could* („konnte“). Sie steht vor allem in verneinten Sätzen und Fragen und mit Verben der Wahrnehmung *(see, hear, ...)*.

GF 13 Reflexive pronouns ▸ *GF pp. 162–163*

'School's out' is an old song – my dad taught **himself** the lyrics when he was still at high school.

Reflexivpronomen *(himself, ourselves, themselves, ...)* bezeichnen dieselbe Person oder Sache wie das Subjekt *(my dad, we, they, ...)*:

Subjekt		Reflexivpronomen	
My dad	*taught*	*himself*	*the lyrics.*
We	*will send*	*ourselves*	*to paradise.*

Mein Vater brachte sich den Text bei.
Wir werden uns ins Paradies schicken.

Reflexive pronouns

Singular		Plural	
myself	(ich) mir/mich	**ourselves**	(wir) uns
yourself	(du) dir/dich	**yourselves**	(ihr) euch
himself	(er) sich	**themselves**	(sie) sich
herself	(sie) sich		
itself	(er/sie/es) sich		

Listen and **relax**! **Imagine** a sunny day on the beach. How does it **feel**?

! Es gibt eine Reihe von Verben, die im Deutschen mit „sich“ gebraucht werden, im Englischen aber ohne Reflexivpronomen.

Beispiele:	
(to) argue	sich streiten
(to) feel	sich (an)fühlen
(to) imagine sth.	sich etwas vorstellen
(to) relax	sich entspannen

GF 14 Reflexive pronoun or *each other*? ▸ *GF p. 163*

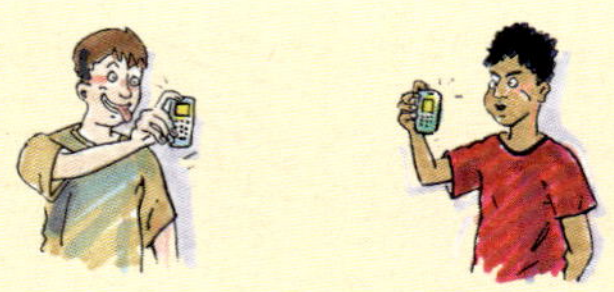

Robert and Asif are taking photos of themselves.
Robert und Asif machen Fotos von sich (selbst).

Für **„sich“** im Sinne von **„sich selbst“** benutzt du die Pronomen auf ***-self/-selves***:
I – myself, we – ourselves, they – themselves usw.

Robert und Asif machen Fotos von sich selbst – Robert fotografiert sich selbst, und Asif fotografiert sich selbst.

Now they are taking photos of each other.
Jetzt fotografieren sie sich gegenseitig. /
Jetzt machen sie Fotos voneinander.

Für **„sich“** im Sinne von **„sich gegenseitig“** oder **„einander“** benutzt du ***each other***.

Robert und Asif fotografieren sich gegenseitig – Robert fotografiert Asif, und Asif fotografiert Robert.

(Statt *each other* wird auch *one another* verwendet:
Now they are taking photos of one another.)

GF 15 Extra Conditional sentences (type 3) ▸ *GF p. 164*

c) Conditional sentences (type 3)

Asif — If Katrina **had come** to London,
I **would have shown** her the sights.
Wenn Katrina nach London **gekommen wäre**,
hätte ich ihr die Sehenswürdigkeiten **gezeigt**.

Bedingungssätze vom Typ 3 sind
„Was wäre gewesen, wenn …"-Sätze.
Sie beziehen sich auf die **Vergangenheit**.
Sie drücken aus, was **geschehen** oder **nicht geschehen wäre**, wenn eine Bedingung eingetreten wäre.

If Katrina had come to London, …

◂ Der ***if*-Satz** nennt eine Bedingung, die nicht eingetreten ist: Katrina ist nicht nach London gekommen.

… Asif would have shown her the sights.

◂ Der **Hauptsatz** drückt aus, was geschehen wäre oder hätte sein können, wenn die Bedingung eingetreten wäre: Wenn Katrina nach London gekommen wäre, dann hätte Asif ihr die Sehenswürdigkeiten zeigen können.

– Im ***if*-Satz** steht das ***past perfect***: *had come.*
– Im **Hauptsatz** steht
***would* + *have* + Partizip Perfekt**: *would have shown.*

If she'd **come** … = If she had **come** …
… he'd **have shown** … = … he would **have shown**

! Beachte:
Die Kurzform *'d* steht im *if*-Satz für *had*,
im Hauptsatz aber für *would*.

If Mika hadn't taken singing lessons,
he couldn't **have sung** at the opera.
Wenn Mika nicht Gesangsstunden genommen hätte,
hätte er nicht an der Oper singen können.

Im Hauptsatz können statt ***would have* + *past participle*** auch ***could have*** oder ***might have* + *past participle*** stehen.

Illustrationen

Roland Beier, Berlin (S. 10; S. 19; S. 24 unten; S. 26; S. 31 oben; S. 32; S. 37; S. 45; S. 47; S. 51; S. 53; S. 59; S. 64; S. 68; S. 71; S. 73–86); Graham-Cameron Illustrations, UK: Fliss Cary (S. 58); Constanze Schargan, Berlin (S. 11; S. 17; S. 22; S. 24 Bild 1–6; S. 25; S. 30; S. 31 unten; S. 56; S. 67; S. 69)

Bildquellen

action press, Hamburg (S. 70: All Action); Alamy, Abingdon (S. 5 li.: PhotosIndia.com LLC; S. 7 Bild 3: Cloe Johnson, Bild 4: Ashley Cooper; S. 8 fans: Liz Boyd, Brick Lane: Marion Bull, Trocadero: Andrew Holt, Science Museum: Mike Booth; S. 12: Travelshots.com; S. 13 oben re.: Blend Images; S. 14 Bild 2: Corbis RF; S. 16 Bild A: The Natural History Museum, Bild D: Bettina Strenske; S. 17 unten re.: Peter Forsberg; S. 25: JUPITERIMAGES/BananaStock; S. 28: f1 online/sodapix; S. 29 unten li.: Photodisc/Malcolm Fife; S. 49: ACE STOCK LIMITED; S. 52 Jessica: RubberBall/Mike Kemp, Jordan: david sanger photography, Ashley: Geoff du Feu; S. 66 Bild 1: PhotosIndia.com LLC); John Birdsall Social Issues Photolibrary, Nottingham (S. 1–2; S. 5 re.; S. 6 Bild 2 u. 3; S. 7 Bild 5; S. 18; S. 27; S. 38; S. 52 Robert; S. 66 Bild 2 u. 3; S. 68); Corbis, Düsseldorf (S. 29 unten re.: Atlantide Phototravel/Massimo Borchi); Jennifer Seidl, München (S. 9 oben; S. 11 oben; S. 14 Bild 1 u. 3; S. 16 Bild C u. F; S. 40; S. 43); Shutterstock, New York (S. 6 Bild 1: Stuart Miles; Bild 4: Tracy Whiteside; S. 7 Bild 1 (M) violin case: Laura Frenkel, bags: maxstockphoto, Bild 2: Vivek Agrawal; S. 8 London Eye: photogl; S. 9 unten re.: Axel Wolf; S. 11 unten: Bryan Busovicki; S. 13 oben li.: Konstantin Sutyagin, oben Mitte: mihaicalin, unten li.: Stephen Bonk, unten Mitte: Andrey Shadrin, unten re.: Tracy Whiteside; S. 14 Bild 4: Darko Novakovic, Bild 5: Joy Brown, Bild 6: Andrey Khrolenok, Bild 7: Losevsky Pavel; S. 16 Bild B u. E: Michal Rosak, Bild G: Jonathan Feinstein; S. 17 oben: WH Chow, Mitte: martin garnham, unten li.: Tyler Boyes, unten Mitte: Andy Lindon; S. 23: Mark Burrows (Nottingham, UK); S. 29 oben: R. Gino Santa Maria; S. 31 Bild 1: Marco Regalia, Bild 2: Guy Erwood, Bild 3: Tischenko Irina, Bild 4: Peter Clark, Bild 5: vladimir maravic, Bild 6: Trutta55; S. 44 British flag (u. 60): Chris Harvey, German flag (u. 60): Kurt De Bruyn, girl: Anthony Monterotti, boy: Magdalena Bujak; S. 48 li.: kavram, re: vera bongaerts; S. 50: John Czenke; S. 52 Bild 1: Gelpi, Bild 2: Andrey Shadrin, Bild 3: Andresr, Bild 4: Elena Elisseeva, Bild 5: Jason Stitt; S. 55: marianad; S. 60 unten: Natalia Bratslavsky; S. 65: Zoom Team); Transport for London, London (S. 9 unten li.)

Titelbild

Alamy, Abingdon (London Eye (M): Ian MacPherson); Corbis, Düsseldorf (bus (M): Royalty-Free); IFA-Bilderteam, Ottobrunn (Union Jack: Jon Arnold Images)